UP THE INFINITE CORRIDOR

Up the Infinite Corridor

MIT AND THE TECHNICAL IMAGINATION

Fred Hapgood

A William Patrick Book

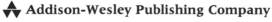 Addison-Wesley Publishing Company

Reading, Massachusetts   Menlo Park, California   New York
Don Mills, Ontario   Wokingham, England   Amsterdam
Bonn   Sydney   Singapore   Tokyo   Madrid   San Juan   Paris   Seoul
Milan   Mexico City   Taipei

Many of the designations used by manufacturers and sellers to distinguish their products are claimed as trademarks. Where those designations appear in this book and Addison-Wesley was aware of a trademark claim, the designations have been printed in initial capital letters (e.g., Frisbee).

Library of Congress Cataloging-in-Publication Data

Hapgood, Fred.
     Up the infinite corridor : MIT and the technical imagination /
Fred Hapgood.
          p.   cm.
     Includes bibliographical references and index.
     ISBN 0-201-08293-4
     1. Massachusetts Institute of Technology. 2. Engineering—United
States—History. I. Title.
T171.M49H37   1993
620'.007207446—dc20   92-31683
                                                                CIP

Jacket design © 1992 by Miriam Ahmed
Text design by Jean Hammond
Set in 11-point New Aster by Publication Services, Inc.

1 2 3 4 5 6 7 8 9-MA-9695949392
First printing, December 1992

To my brother,
Will Hapgood,
who knew and knows
where to find the center

CONTENTS

Caveats ix

Acknowledgments xi

1 Solution Space 1

2 The Infinite Corridor 13

3 A Different Variety of Mind 25

4 The Architecture of Solution Space 47

5 Engineering Science 63

6 The Tech Model Railroad Club 89

7 The MIT Knee 109

8 The Media Lab 129

9 Nanotechnology 145

10 Technical Sports 157

11 The Vision Chip 173

Selected Bibliography 193

Index 197

CAVEATS

Fundamentally, this book is about engineering: the flow of the enterprise, the character of its imagination, the nature of its relation to the world. There is more to MIT than engineering—the best economics department in America; the best museum of contemporary art in Boston—and I apologize to all the organs of the Institute ignored here. Second, the version of the relation between the history of American engineering and MIT presented herein was absorbed from materials collected by the Institute and interviews with historians in the community. Other engineering schools will no doubt detect a certain bias, and no doubt they will be right. Eventually, some heroic scholar will write a measured, neutral history of American engineering that assigns the right degree of influence, and the right fraction of historical contribution to all the actors. This book is just the view from one institution.

The thorniest question I faced in writing this text was figuring out how and whether to address the excellent odds that the sex ratio of the profession is due to change dramatically. For the present, MIT is still very male, at least on the level (graduate school) with which I was mostly concerned. However, the undergraduate school is almost 50/50, and presumably the ratios of the graduate school and faculty will soon fall into line. Ultimately, I decided to take the institution as it is rather than as it probably will be.

ACKNOWLEDGMENTS

MIT is impressive along many dimensions, but the quality that has touched me most often since I first walked into the Institute is its generosity of access: all up and down the corridors the doors stand open, and whomever I interviewed always brought as much and usually more effort to the labor of clarifying the subject as I did. Terrible advantage was taken of this tradition; I can only hope I did not leave it fatally discredited. In addition to those mentioned specifically in the text, I am left in debt to H. Kent Bowen, Nancy Daly, Rick Danheiser, Jim Davis, Randy Duran, Tom Eager, Woodie Flowers, Simson Garfinkle, Paul Gray, Chris Hable, Mikkio Hakkaranen, David Hardt, Alan Hatton, Ricky Hessdorfer, Ron Hoffman, Bertold Horn, Larry Jones, Craig Keast, Jay Keyser, Alan Kotek, David Lampe, Minos Leodidas,

Jim Leonard, Timothy McGovern, Ignacio McQuirk, Kathy Marquis, Fred Mikkelsen, Andy Miller, Crispin Miller, Chad Mirkin, Mike Mornard, Susan Murcott, Russ Neuman, James Nowick, Bill Onorato, Mike Patton, Tommaso Poggio, John Purbrick, Mitch Resnick, Dan Roos, Robert Rose, Mike Rosen, Mark Seidel, John Shields, William Siebert, David Small, Chris Stacey, David Sturman, John Underkoffler, David Gorden Wilson, Gerry Wilson, and David Zeltzer. Rob Sanner and Harry West were tireless in their willingness to keep reseating me on the right track. Outside the MIT community I found I could ask Dave Lindbergh, Jerry Roberts, Bob Hawkins, and my engineer brother, Will Hapgood, anything I wanted in perfect confidence that I would get a provocative and precise answer before I was halfway through the question. Vin McLellan, Mark Kramer, Tracy Kidder, Carolyn May, Richard Conte, and Susan Goldhor read the manuscript and pointed out how I might ameliorate its failings. The reader can judge how far I took their advice. Finally, my wife, Susan, showed me how to find and hold on to what matters, both in the page and outside it.

UP THE INFINITE CORRIDOR

ONE

Solution Space

In his time Ernesto Blanco has designed robot arms, a lens
for cataract operations, steerable catheters (that can navigate inside arterial branches), a microstapler for eye surgery, a stair-climbing wheelchair, a forklift truck, film-processing equipment, high-voltage transmission line
connectors, a helium pump, and a raft of devices for the
textile industry—from pile stitchers to faulty needle sensors.
So he has earned the right, which he exercises, to dress his
barrel chest and ramrod carriage in rich blue blazers and
snowy shirt linens, silk ties, Italian leathers, and flawlessly
creased flannels. In this he faces against the winds of fashion
at MIT, where an Armani suit suggests not success or
achievement but a serious problem with self-esteem, a lack
of confidence that the product, the work, will be adequate to

win the desired rewards. The psychology expresses itself in a fashion paradox: at MIT you dress up, you dress for success, by dressing down. So in this sense Blanco is like a banker who wears jeans to work; he is good enough to wear what he likes, and what he likes is Fifth Avenue.

One day Blanco's niece appealed to this same expansive confidence by asking her uncle if he could figure out a way that she could turn the sheets on a music stand without taking her hands off her instrument. Well, of course, Blanco said, but not immediately; he had responsibilities, a schedule. He had a company (textile machinery) to run. He wouldn't be able to get it done for a couple weeks at the earliest.

In the first spare moment he had, the engineer built a straightforward imitation of human paging, a linkage that dragged a rubber knob across the page from right to left when the musician pressed a foot pedal. The theory underlying the device was simple enough: when the coefficient of friction between knob and page was greater than that between the top page and the page just underneath, the top page would move. Unfortunately, the same theory held for the second page down, and the third, so if the knob pressed down one degree too hard, the pager would flip two or three pages over at once. One degree too light, of course, and it wouldn't turn even one page. Further, the coefficient of friction of paper is affected by dirt, wrinkles, the texture and coatings of the paper, even the humidity, so the exact amount of pressure required had to be readjusted for each new piece of music or performance. In fact, the correct pressure might change even during a performance, since some bindings impress different forces on the top page and the last.

In any case, a practical self-paging music stand would have to do more than move paper; it had to be cheap to buy, operate, and maintain, quiet, highly dependable, simple to use, light, compatible with ordinary sheet music, and reasonably attractive. (Also, since Blanco was volunteering his labor, the cost of design had to be low.) Friction-driven paging solved the primary problem, but it lost on the dependability end. Blanco knew that a great deal of work might squeeze enough design sophistication into the pager to force performance to an acceptable level, but then you would have started to bleed along the cost, ease-of-use, and maintenance dimensions. His bones told him that frictional paging was a dead end.

Hmm. If humans weren't a good model, how about machines? How do the paper-handling machines in the paper and printing industry and in copiers work? Suction! Of course! What these machines did was drop little tubes down on the sheets, pump the air out of the tubes, and use the difference in pressure on either side of the sheet to pick it up. The design flowed into his mind in a moment. The foot pedal would swing a suction tube over the page, the tube would drop, and enough air would be drawn from the tube to lift the page through a 90-degree arc. "This is beautiful," Blanco remembers saying to himself. So simple. This is what engineering is about. He went out and got a violin stand.

The machine model turned out to be not that much more useful. Air flows through paper so readily that small differences in pressure quickly disappear. Industrial paper-handlers work because they have enough power to suck air faster than it can be replenished from the other side of the sheet, and developing that much power from a foot pedal made the pager impractically hard to use. An electrically powered air compressor would have worked and therefore might have solved the dependability problem (though the porosity of paper is very hard to predict), but only by violating the cost and weight and probably the noise constraints. A foot-operated suction pump could move plastic sheets, but a practical pager obviously had to work with ordinary paper sheet music. Requiring the musician to transfer sheet music to a nonporous medium before the performance would have made the device impossibly complicated.

Uncle Blanco started pouring more hours into the project. He next looked at inserting wires or strips of metal at each page and then lifting the page through the required arc by lifting the strip. This was dependable and cheap and light and quiet, but the musician had to preload the system by inserting the wires or strips ahead of time, and that made the stand too cumbersome. He tried using sticky tape on a swinging arm to pick up the sheets. This satisfied the power constraint, but it failed the nondestructiveness test: when the arm pulled the tape back off the page either the paper tore or the stickum on the tape came off on the paper, gumming up the music. Finally, he reached the end of the road. There were just so many ways to tie up the package, and each left some essential features lying on the ground. "I just gave up," Blanco said. "I decided to dump the whole thing."

In a word, Professor Blanco was stuck. In *Zen and the Art of Motorcycle Maintenance*, Robert Persig, perhaps the first to sense and explore the spiritual deeps of engineering, insists that "stuckness" is the key, the heart of the process, "the very void Zen Buddhists go to so much trouble to induce through koans, deep breathing, sitting still . . . " Any nontrivial act of design (and not a few seemingly trivial ones, like a no-hands music pager) can bring you here, empty you out, rip away your confidence in your own notions, your worldview, your metaphysics, leave you out on the tundra without the least idea which direction to take.

When this happens, when a person is exhausted and demoralized and under enormous pressure and not only has no idea what to do next but has given up all hope of even having a new idea, the ego will sometimes relax, will allow its prisoner a few seconds of direct observation of what is sitting right in front of his face. While legend speaks of some mystics and masters—like Boethius or the great electrical engineer Charles Steinmetz—who could stare at unvarnished reality for hours at a time, for most of us the ego reasserts its claims over perception in minutes, seconds. Still, it is the promise of such experiences, though rare and hard-won, that brings in the recruits.

Anyway, Blanco couldn't forget the problem. He felt more than frustrated; he felt humiliated. He would sit at his desk and push the pages of a book of music back and forth, admiring the simplicity of the process, the choreography of the sheets, watching them flutter and riffle. A book would display two pages to the world, then, with just an ounce of force, just by rotating a single sheet of paper around a single edge, two new faces would appear. It was a beautiful and elegant process. Why couldn't he do it? Obviously there was a way. He must be an idiot. He had no business calling himself an engineer. Why hadn't he become a lawyer when he had a chance? Now it was too late. . . .

The fluttering pages rose and fell. Maybe someday someone else, someone smarter, will see the right way to do this. That would be nice. The world could use a device like this. I wonder if it will be in my lifetime? Wish I knew what it will be. Probably not lifting the pages with wires or ribbons; it's just too hard to load the system. Probably not friction or suction. The problems with those approaches are just too obvious. More than likely the right idea will use adhesiveness somehow; some smart person will see how to use adhesion without ruining the paper. Good luck to them. Blanco took a length of Scotch tape and wrapped it idly around his finger, sticky-side out, and began picking up the pages with it. Look how easy it is. Even my finger can do it; why can't I?

Then, like a lens suddenly twisting into focus, Blanco noticed what his finger was doing: it wasn't ripping free from a turned page; it was *peeling* free by rotating against the page. He picked up another page and rotated his finger; the page peeled off and fell back, leaving no mark, no tear, no pieces of adhesive. Press, lift, turn, peel; press, lift, turn, peel. His stupidity hit him like a body blow. Of course! When you try to pull tape off a piece of paper by pulling straight up, perpendicular to the page, as his last device had, the tensile forces are resisted by the whole area of the tape stuck to the paper. The only way to get the tape free is to put so much force into the act that you end up damaging the materials. But if you bend the tape all the way around, 180 degrees, so it is parallel to the paper, and then pull it, the tensile forces become concentrated along the edge of the connection between tape and paper. You can get the same separation with less force and, therefore, with less damage.

There the answer had been all this time, literally under his nose, waving, calling out, throwing pebbles at his bedroom window, honking on the street. Blanco got no sense of satisfaction from his discovery; there had been no dazzling insights or feats of creativity. "I was disgusted with myself," he said. The entirety of his achievement was that he had peeped out between his fingers at the real world for a bare second, and been forced to remember what he should never have forgotten: the difference between peeling and ripping. You shouldn't hand yourself any ribbons for that.

This was not a new experience to Blanco; as a professional engineer he knew that the great shredding of the ego happens with every design of any interest, though the trauma grows no less painful than stage fright does for a professional actor. Each year Blanco gives a lecture on the process to MIT sophomores, a description of the sacrifices that will be exacted by their prospective profession. He stands up in his splendid threads, holding a signboard with a spiral, a whirlpool, an illustration of the pit of frustration down which they will be asked to fling themselves again and again. This doesn't just come with the territory, Blanco says, it is the territory. If the moment comes when you can no longer bear to see just how stupid you really are, when you think you know so much you no longer need to be clubbed into opening your eyes, then it is time to pass into the gray outbox of the engineering profession. It is time to go into management.

Humans and computers alike solve simple problems with clear-cut procedures that lead directly to the final answer, like following a road map. More complex problems are solved by interactively generating some candidate solutions, fine-tuning the solver with their experience, and then making some more candidates, over and over. The better chess-playing computers constantly change their move-picking strategies according to how other moves have succeeded. A "traveling salesman" program trying to define the shortest route connecting a group of cities does so by sampling possible itineraries and refining its search procedure accordingly. Biological species adapt by accumulating and reorganizing genetic specializations acquired from prior lives in other environments. Decision and systems theorists sometimes refer to these volumes of plausible answers as "solution spaces," and problem-solving, defining paths through these volumes, as "searching" solution space.

Engineering can also be seen as a family of paths crossing a solution space—in this case a space defined by all the possible arrangements and combinations of geometry, time, and material properties that might satisfy the particular specifications of a design. Filtering a good design out of these possibilities by simple, direct calculation is impossible both because of the enormous number of variables and because there are always elements in the specifications—like aesthetics or ergonomics or compatibility with the corporate image—that can't be reduced to a number or folded into a common denominator. What humans do in these cases is what Blanco did: think up a completely wrong (but sincerely felt) approach to the problem, jump in, fail, and then do an autopsy. Each failure contains encrypted somewhere on its body directions for the next jump: "strengthen this part," "tie this down next time," "buy a better battery." Good engineering is not a matter of creativity or centering or grounding or inspiration or lateral thinking, as useful as those might be, but of decoding the clever, even witty, messages solution space carves on the corpses of the ideas in which you believed with all your heart, and then building the road to the next message.

In the 1970s a British industrialist named Henry Kremer established a prize for the first airplane that could take off under human power and fly for a mile. (Kremer was a physical fitness enthusiast and is said to have been possessed by the vision of British youth pedaling through the skies to manly vigor.) The idea was not entirely new—occasionally pedal-powered propellers had been screwed onto gliders—but the performance of such devices had never amounted to much, because humans produce very little power per pound of body weight: much less than a bird or insect, let alone the smallest gasoline-powered motor. In theory wing area can compensate for power, but humans are too weak to lift a wing design with anything close to even a glider's weight per square foot. The engineering challenge was therefore to design a structure that had lots of wing and a total weight half that of the pilot, was robust enough to survive the stresses of real flight, and could be built for volunteer levels of time and money. In short, a hard nut, and a number of very heavy theory shops— MIT, Cal Tech, the University of Tokyo—jumped right in.

The team that won was none of these but a group of hobbyists, directed by a businessman named Paul Ma- Cready, who compensated for their supposed deficiencies in theory by evolving a design that tolerated repair, and tolerated it generously. Because the *Gossamer Albatross* could be repaired cheaply and quickly, it could be stressed to failure, pushed until it crashed, over and over. Each of these experiments—you couldn't really call them accidents—was a highly context-sensitive tutorial in the trade-offs possible among strength, weight, and cost. When a part failed, either by breaking or, since strength has to be paid for with weight, *not* breaking, that failure did much more than testify to an inadequacy in the original design: the timing, severity, and path of the failure underlined the issue needing attention next and pointed suggestively in the direction of a likely solution. By the time the group claimed the Kremer prize, the plane had crashed five hundred times. Had they had the time to let it crash a thousand, the *Albatross* might have flown for a week.

This is the fundamental cycle, the atom of the process, the unit of movement in solution space. In formal contexts the process is known as generate-and-test or design- through-debugging or guided iteration; among themselves engineers call it tinkering or trial-and-error. The develop- ment of any given tool—the ax, the automobile, the com- puter—grows out of thousands of these cycles, as tissue is composed of cells. Even taken as no more than a metaphor, the phrase at least resonates with the terms of motion those inside the corridors use to describe their life: the narratives about inching uphill and sliding back down; of being mired in a swamp or trapped at the bottom of a pit or captivated by an interesting side alley or running full tilt into a cliff or tumbling into a nest of venomous glitch demons; of scrutinizing possibilities on the other side of a distance and affirming or rejecting them for reasons that might fail on a "closer" look; of being on the wave; and of being stuck.

The more time one spends in the corridors the more intuitive an idea solution space becomes. It grows from seeming like casual jargon to an apt metaphor to an alternate metaphysics to the obviously right way of thinking about the universe. Walking around inside the corridors the differences between subjective and objective, the physical and the psychical, what is and what should be, the artificial and the natural, the discovered and the invented, the given and the created become steadily harder to keep in mind. To engineer means to locate and bring together those bits of nature that have the same interests you do, the same ideas, the same desires; do that well enough, precisely enough, often enough, and the tremendous differences we think exist between the material and imaginative realms begin to fade away.

Sometimes the ideas arise inside us and organize their mirror image from natural properties; sometimes the process seems to start with a natural configuration, like tape peeling from a finger, that leaps into our imagination from "outside." From the perspective of solution space it sometimes seems (no doubt this is an illusion) that we force ourselves into solution space no more than we are carried; that we are building what this universe wants us to build, when it wants us to build it, and it just doesn't matter how stupid we are, the Lord be thanked. After all, is it plausible that creatures as shallow, slow, blind, and distractible as human beings could build anything as complicated as a cloverleaf overpass without guidance?

Solution Space

Years ago an engineer told me a fantasy he thought threw some light on the ends of engineering, or at least on those underlying his own labors. A flying saucer arrives on Earth and the crew starts flying over cities and dams and canals and highways and grids of power lines; they follow cars on the roads and monitor the emissions of TV towers. They beam up a computer into their saucer, tear it down, and examine it. "Wow," one of them finally exclaims. "Isn't nature incredible!?"

He loved that image: the aliens, sitting in their saucer, waving their pseudopodia in excited awe, just like we do when we really look at the webs of spiders or beehives or the glory of a rainbow or a crystal or the patterns of waves on the sea. That's what he built for, he said, not just for his clients or even for himself but to stun the aliens, to zap them with awe at the creation.

Several years later I happened to be eating dinner in Santa Fe with a group of programmers. When time came to pay the bill two members of the party were missing. Investigation turned them up hunched over the computer that drove that cash register. One had wanted a copy of the receipt, and on being told this was impossible had asked to take a look at the program so he could see why. One glance and his stomach went into spasm: the program was appalling, a shuddersome mess of "spaghetti code," illogical and inefficient and ugly and dangerous—full of booby traps cocked and waiting.

His friend had joined him, and the pair asked the rest of us to leave them there. They'd take a taxi or something, but it was impossible to just walk off and leave all that ugliness radiating its disorder and unintelligence into the night air. Next day I ran into one of the party. It had turned out to be a nightmare, he said; the register program was written in a language they'd last used when they were about 11. The session had gone on for hours. But they'd finished the rewrite, and to this day perhaps the tightest and most elegant piece of cash register code in the entire country is sitting in a restaurant in New Mexico, waiting to stun the aliens.

The Infinite Corridor

Viewed from the air, the bulk of the MIT campus can be wrapped by a line that runs northeast for a mile along the Cambridge side of the Charles River, angles sharply west up through five blocks of Kendall Square, and then swings southerly for a long run back to the Charles. Near the middle of this triangle, on the eastern edge of a major thoroughfare that bisects the campus, a broad and graceful flight of stairs ripples to the second story of the outer edge of a large, white, U-shaped building. This is the front door of MIT, and the entrance to its most famous architectural feature: an internal road, perhaps 8 feet wide by 15 high, that rolls straight as a plumb line for 762 feet and through five buildings.

An eye sighting down the length of the Infinite Corridor, as this feature is known, will cross dozens of structural ribs dropping from the ceiling or butting out from the walls. To an observer seated at the entrance, perspective so condenses these that the window at the far end looks like a tiny square egg incubating in a nest of right angles. The image hints at intersections, transactions, with dozens of other corridors equally complex, the whole ramifying out into an enormous labyrinth.

An observer moving down the corridor, penetrating the matrix, might be struck first of all by the absence of landmarks. The same modular building sections lead off from every intersection; the same uniform array of doors runs down every wall. The walls, in general a single shade of beige, as though the entire Institute had been painted out of the same paint can, are strikingly unmarked and unornamented for a university campus. When a corridor passes into a building—most of the buildings at MIT are connected by a grid of corridors, walkways, and tunnels—note of that fact might be marked with a slim strip of wood or stripe of paint, but then again it might not. Few areas are set apart by the special color schemes or posters that usually guard the borders of departmental territories. Every open door reveals the same equipment racks and computer workstations and desks piled with a chaos of paper.

The sense of interchangeability is dramatized by the convention of addressing the buildings by number, not name: Building 3, Building 10, as if they were just larger rooms in a single enormous building. No neighborhoods are defined even by that colorless terminology: Building 7 feeds into 3 and 3 sits next to 10 and 10 next to 4, and so on. A stranger rushing to make a scheduled appointment might think the design calculated to drive him crazy, but a visitor free to wander might also be impressed by the freedom of direction, the unpredictability of association, the richness of interconnection. Any point in the campus seems equally near or far from any other. The same degree of associative freedom might be felt in wandering through the consciousness of an exceptionally vital mind.

The conversations overheard in the corridors have the same quality of diversity-in-uniformity. The conversations take off from any point at all—from this planet or another, from inside a molecule or as a cognition running in software, from the perspective of a character in a computer game or an arthritic knee or a robot struggling to clean windows—and reach out in any direction you can care to imagine. They are alike offhand, amused, and fast; the speakers sound less as if they were thinking their way through the subject than reading text scrolling through their minds at about four words a second. The speaker-listener roles bounce back and forth with the pace of a racquet sport. To an observer listening *through* the content, listening to the music, the rhythms of these exchanges seem as adapted and familiar and enmeshed as that of spouses in an old marriage.

"I've been thinking about quality displays," a student sitting next to me in the cafeteria says to her classmate. "And I've just about decided that you really have to have stereo." (By which the speaker means putting slightly different images into the right and left eyes so as to get the illusion of depth.)

"I suppose the simplest way to do that would be to have eyephones," says her tablemate.

"Eyephones?"

"Yeah." The second speaker clasps his hands into tubes and cups them over his eyes.

"Ah," the first speaker says. "Another would be to construct every pixel out of hundreds of little lenses on gimbals. Then every ray of light could be transmitted in all possible directions."

"But could you pipe that much power through a single pixel?"

"If not, maybe the viewer could wear a marker that would tell the display where his eyes were. Then the rays could be sent to just the right spots. A display like that would run on even less power than the ones we use now."

"But suppose several people were watching?" the second replies. (His meaning being, could the rays be beamed into several pairs of eyes simultaneously.) "I still think eyephones are the way to go."

"But consider the problem with reflective surfaces."

"Reflective surfaces? What problem?"

"Well, when you look at a good reflective surface you see your face in it. Good displays will eventually have to have cameras so they can put your face in mirrors or whatever. Do you want to see eyephones hanging out of your face?"

Perhaps the point of view most useful for meditating on the culture of the Institute begins with locating the varieties of human sensitivity along a dimension running from the psychology of wholes to the physics of parts. The former feels behavior, whether of mechanical or biological actors, as something that emerges from the whole, as an expression of the will of the whole pulling the present toward some state imagined and desired by the whole. The latter feels behavior as coming from the interactions of parts pushing the whole "from behind," through the rearrangement of past states. The "physics" that is relevant to the former is called psychology, and is constructed of whole-oriented processes like feelings and wishes and intentions and desires.

The "psychology" that is relevant to the latter is called physics, and is built up out of the dynamics that comprise cause-and-effect. Somebody who sees the entire universe as a psyche writ large, pulsing with feelings and intentions and consciousness, in short, lies on one extreme; such a person will have no patience with talk about the laws of conservation or symmetry or causality, the amorality of natural processes, or the illusory nature of free will, since such considerations come from the domain of parts. A sternly reductive scientist, for whom the only realities flow out of the rearrangement of past states, sits at the other end of the table; he or she will be endlessly skeptical that there is any fact or effect in the universe, including "life" and "consciousness," for which conclusively adequate accounts cannot be woven from the cascade of historical causes.

Each of us, engineers included, are bent one way or the other, but only engineers have a professional duty to straddle this divide. Engineers build tools (a chair is a tool, a road is a tool), and tools connect these domains, combining as they do intentions and physical properties, cause-and-effect and will, the interaction of parts and the unified assertion of the whole, the conserved properties of the past and the decidedly unconserved dynamics of wishes, whims, and dreams. Tools are an integration-in-hardware of the two realms.

The technical name for wishes is "specifications," examples of which might be speed, grace, ergonomics, ease of use, stability, low manufacturing costs, fun, fantasy, and the subversion of the established order, perhaps by writing an encryption program tough enough to give the National Security Agency hives. Over there in the other realm are physical properties, parameters: mechanics, materials, chemistry, electronics, magnetism, optics, and the power of algorithms. Joining the two means developing a field of connections that spreads out through both domains, interactively changing

what is to be asked for and can be given, what is felt and
known on each level. MIT is a culture of connections and
connecting. All the aspects of science and society flow
through the corridors, combining, separating, and recom-
bining; its humor and heroes and traumas are alike fruit
from this tree. The pleasure the members take in obscure
varieties of puns: unit-of-measure puns, like giving their age
in days or their address in polar coordinates (Joke: "What's
the unit of beauty?" "The millihelen, or enough beauty to
launch one ship."), or in logical puns ("Are you coming or
staying here?" "Yes.") mocks this focus on mixing, combining, shuffling, connecting. Once during a lecture the issue
arose of the nature of creativity in engineering. "The best
engineer I ever knew," the professor, Harry West, said,
"never had an original idea in his life. All he'd do—*all he'd
do*—is go around and talk to people, and then . . ." here West
swung his arms out toward the incline of seats, meshed his
fingers together, and lifted his voice ". . . then he'd put it
all together." "Was he being 'creative'?" he cried out to his
audience.

"**I** see MIT as a surfing contest," a graduate student once
said. "When you're on the wave, you're moving as fast as
you will anywhere in the world. But . . ." he lifted a skeletal
index finger up and staked it in the air, ". . . anything can
wipe you out." The trip wires are everywhere. The very next
problem in the problem set could turn out to be undecipher-
able; the next lecture, impenetrable; the next course, coun-
terintuitive and bizarre. You could work for a year on a
high-quality display, only to find at the end that it is so good,
so clever, that it makes the consumers feel ugly (because it
shows eyephones hanging out of their eyes). Any design
problem can turn at any point into a "rubber wall bug"—a

glitch that sucks nourishment out of all your efforts to correct it, growing ever fatter and more evil until it bounces you totally out of the design and back to zero. In short, at any moment another horrid cycle of the great shredding of the ego can come out of nowhere and grab you off.

Every institution has a certain range of acts that illuminate and amplify its cultural essence (in the view of some fraction of the population)—hazing incidents in fraternities, corruption in legislatures, price fixing by businesses, etc. At MIT these are suicides. Though the administration insists that no more students actually go through with the act than is "normal"—one in ten thousand per year—for adolescents, the reverberations of each actual case spread through the campus and the surrounding community for days. General interest reporters, who privately suspect that all that math would make anyone suicidal, never tire of playing up the "cost of excellence" angle, with its reassuring subtext about the dangers of working hard in school. "It's the John Wayne mentality, writ large," one associate dean for student affairs said in an interview. "Students put a lot of pressure on themselves here. . . . This drive to be the best—that's America. And let's face it. You don't do it—you don't understand the mechanism of superconductivity—by working eight-hour days and spending a lot of time around the fireplace with the kids."

Inside the culture, the salience of suicide is seen not as a function of any internally generated "John Wayne mentality, writ large" but as the product of the environment, of the risk, to which everyone is vulnerable, of being thrown off balance and swept behind, of being lost in the torrent. Once I was casually exchanging weird facts with a graduate student and mentioned that most people who shoot themselves in the head miss. "Right!" he said instantly. "And do you know why? Because when they pull the trigger, they jerk."

He stuck two fingers in his mouth and pantomimed the error. "They pull their heads back. But there's a way around that! When you put the gun in, you have to lock your teeth over the front sight, then if you jerk your head, the gun goes with you!" He slammed his thumb down on the firing chamber and yanked his head back. "That's how you do it." Up to this point he'd been bantering with me, but here his tone gathered weight and grew more intent. "If you learn anything at MIT, it's how to commit suicide." You learn which toxicology texts have the real stuff and how much weight should be placed where on the body to make sure that a leap from a given height will not merely injure and the details of a quality connection between flesh and electricity and the water intake per pound required to trigger a fatal disruption in the ionic balance of the cells.

A few years ago an undergraduate arrived with the rare custom of expressing general approval and contentment by mooing like a cow. (This had been a private family joke.) Eventually he forgot himself and "mooed" at school. To his surprise, instead of ridiculing him, the other students thought that was really witty, that mooing was totally apt, exactly what was needed, and they picked up the practice. Soon mooing was heard all over his dorm, and here and there in the larger campus, in the lecture halls and library stacks. The members of his dorm renamed the geography of the Institute to reflect pasture and dairy motifs, linguistically transforming the campus into a bucolic sweep of copses and meadows and rolling knolls and streams; they invented handshakes and instituted dietary practices based on milk. They printed up T-shirts and compiled canonical lists of herd puns. Initially, membership in the herd was entirely by self-election, but as interest spread questions arose about the proper definitions of herd ritual and the geographic limits of the concept. Could anybody just be a member of the herd, whoever they were, whatever they did? How about Reverend Moon or Pol Pot? A constitutional convention was held, the anarchist and libertarian factions combined forces, and in a triumph of radical inclusiveness membership in the herd was thrown open to the world.

"I was happy to be part of that," the student said later. "I felt it gave us a little of the feeling of what it meant to be in college." Students at MIT use the phrase "being in college" to refer to the experiences they feel they denied themselves by coming here, in this case the pleasures of being slow and passive and purposeless and undifferentiated, of being content to be a solid block of warm meat with an intellectual life barely above that of domesticated corn. There may well be institutions of higher education in the country that come close enough to this description, but probably the contribution made by the herd was just as intrinsic to an MIT education as calculus. The students were freeing each other to float idly on the waves, belly to the sun, and let the connections roar by.

Perhaps the most advanced level of adaptation accepts the humor of being chronically, if marginally, off balance, and actually speeds up, embracing the experience of this psychedelic tumbling, these episodes of disorientation. Ordinarily this state of mind expresses itself in technical pursuits, but there are more accessible contexts, such as the popular dances sponsored by TechSquares, the MIT square-dancing association. These dances draw on an enormous vocabulary of calls, up to a few thousand, all of which a dancer (at that level) is expected to know. Some calls involve imaginary or "virtual" dancers, so-called "phantom spots," that give the choreographer 12 or 16 centers of motion instead of 8. Many calls break the ring into two concentric rings of four dancers that move quasi-independently, with the dancers of each ring giving a different interpretation to each call. (Unlike traditional calls, these are not gender-specific. There are no calls whose execution varies with the sex of the dancer. This permits squares with unequal sex ratios, like six males and two females, though when equal numbers are available the dancers pair up in the traditional way.)

Planning the sequences is a demanding art, almost always requiring a computer, and new sequences are required constantly; the experience loses its edge, or so dancers say, unless the series of calls is completely unpredictable. The challenge to the dancers is to keep the square going, to keep the group spinning and folding and unfolding as the caller jumps back and forth inside this huge volume of possibilities. If one dancer out of the eight takes more than perhaps a half-second to identify, remember, and execute the call, the square will collapse. The ideal is for the caller and eight dancers to bring each square to the edge of collapse and keep it balanced there, hanging over the face of the wave.

At the dances I visited the tempo seemed slower than in conventional square dancing, though the caller rattled off a call every two or three seconds: pass the ocean, extend flipback, recycle, ocean wave, horseshoe turn, once removed, dodge circulate, grand cross trade and wheel, chisel through, diagonal box, change the web, and on and on. The dancers less flowed through these calls than walked rapidly, but their step was light, and as the dance proceeded it seemed to get lighter. Whenever the square collapsed a burst of laughter flew up to the ceiling. This happened often enough that it came to seem part of the dance itself, almost as if the intensity one saw on the dancers' faces reflected not the effort of remembering all these calls but of holding in the laughter as long as possible. Each minute the square survived the smiles grew; one had the sense of eight bubbles of hilarity (per square) expanding continuously, as if these dances were lifting the squares to regions of lower and lower pressure. Then the square would fail, the laughter would escape into the air, the caller would skip a beat, and the square would reform.

At one point in one dance a Kristofferson song, in a version played by the Mustang Boys, was on the turntable, and the caller, a thin, bearded engineer named Don Beck, issued a call that required the dancers to remember some number of calls in the past and repeat the sequence. Don had been calling for almost an hour, and the excitement and the music and laughter from the floor had him soaring. Holding the mike up as if he was draining a bottle of beer, he strutted over the floor while the dancers twisted in front of him like moving vortices, spinning themselves out and reeling themselves back in, bouncing in and out of the center of the square, linking into nested rhombs and counterrotating triangles that passed in and out of each other, clenching and unclenching and coiling and uncoiling over the floor, like eight self-juggling balls throwing each other higher and higher.

THREE

A Different
Variety
of Mind

Hominid societies have been using tools for more than a million years, but not until recently did these amount to more than crudely worked axes and choppers. About 40,000 – 50,000 years ago, for reasons that are still unsettled but probably related to the acquisition of language, in Africa, Europe and Asia alike, awls, chisels, cleavers, discs, gravers, knives, scrapers, anvils, fish hooks, harpoons, lance points, chippers, needles, polishers, spears and spear throwers, canoes, baskets, nets, ceramic pots (which implies kilns), pounders, sickles and saw blades, bows and arrows, hearth ovens, personal ornaments, cosmetics, and hints of clothing begin to be laid down in the stratigraphical columns. The men and women of the late Neolithic built from stone, wood, clay, bone, skin, horn, ivory, and plant fibers; they made compound tools of different materials and subassemblies. They began to draw and make records. They even made "tool art"—knives and choppers too delicate to be practical, but which embodied the spirit and ambitions of tools and toolmaking.

Most of these early tools were small, cheap, and portable (the roots of the throwaway culture run deep). Around the first or second millennium B.C. tools requiring several man-years to construct began to appear: roads, aqueducts, irrigation systems, tunnels, mines, dams, canals, piers, ships and shipyards, fortifications and other structures (like pyramids), siege engines, and smelteries. The cost of these artifacts meant that few could be built, which prevented experience in designing, constructing, and running them from diffusing through the culture in general. They also behaved differently from small tools: a design that works for a building 10 feet high will be a disaster at 50, and vice versa. A person designing a paved road capable of carrying the traffic required to feed a city must face questions about construction and maintenance that would never occur to anyone trimming a foot path. Those responsible for this category of artifact, for following function into peculiar, unfamiliar, contexts where everyday common sense failed, came to be known as engineers.

Until industrialization no country had more than a handful, most billeted to the military. At the turn of the eighteenth century the United States had fewer than most. The number of working steam engines could be counted on the fingers of one hand, and large projects like paved highways, chemical factories, and ironworks were known only from reports of the wonders then unfolding in Europe. The Americans blamed their lack of development on the British, who as masters of the colonies had taken special pains to suppress any possible threat to their manufacturing preeminence. No doubt there were other factors, other explanations. Whatever, over the next 60 years the country, or at least that part of it north of the Mason-Dixon line, dragged itself into modern times.

The historical consensus credits this achievement to a tiny handful of mechanics and engineer/manufacturers, worthies like Eli Whitney, or Sam Colt, or Chauncey Jerome (who started the clock industry). Their numbers sum to a few hundred or at most a thousand. No doubt more tried to respond to the industrial needs of the nation, to dig canals and build locomotives and run power into mills, but building in isolation and out of ignorance, with neither the proper tools nor any accumulated technical lore, is a respectable piece of labor. For most who tried failure came often, and when it did it was catastrophic: a canal wall collapsing, a ton of molten iron falling on a floor. Those who could build structures that stood and machines that ran were different, and knew it, in part because their wages were about as high as wages in those days got. (One canal engineer, working not long after the Revolution, received four times the average annual income of the time for a six-week job, in addition to special allowances for travel time, a servant, and enough meat, cheese, and Madeira to require the hire of three horses.)

The historian of technology Elting Morison wrote of this period:

> *Engineers in those days moved almost always through atmospheres of doubt and controversy. And it did not help very much that the thing that was said to be impossible while they were building was taken, when they had finished, to be a wonder. It is not surprising, therefore, that, having to trust their own private calculations of natural forces amid the incalculable noise of the crowd, they developed in time into independent, austere, and utterly self-confident men.*

"In their letters, anecdotes, and memoirs," he continues, "there is not much humor, less wit, and very little hail-fellow-well-met. What does come through is respect for certain oft-mentioned abstract virtues ... honesty, accuracy, fidelity. One of the type had carved on his tombstone only the word 'Veritas,' and truth in structure is what they had all learned to live by."* Here and there in their memoirs the members of this elite revealed the name of the power that allowed them to empty themselves into the moment, to pick out the flow of changes that counted, to read the meaning of a shift in temperature or intuit a pool of stress building in a shaft or rope; the power that set them apart and touched their small number with success. They called it a sense for "the fitness of things."

A sense for the fitness of things was a gift, like any other extraordinary sense. It could not be taught; the old engineers were quite explicit on this point. Those who had it were engineers in their soul, even if they chose to throw away their legacy by going into law, whereas 30 years in the profession could not make those lacking the gift into engineers. References to this sense are few and those few elliptical, as if any reader who does not already know what is meant is beyond explanation, but passages can be found that seem to touch on the subject indirectly. One is a scene that appears, with variants, in a number of the memoirs left by these old masters. The engineer-to-be, then around 9 or 10, is alone with an adult, perhaps his father or a local mechanic; the adult is absorbed in some intricate task, like reaming out

---

*A line of Francis Bacon's expands on the sentiment: "Works are of greater value as pledges of truth than as contributions to the comforts of life."

a log to make a pipe or building a barrel. No words are spoken, or if they are, they are not remembered. The adult is intent on his labor; the boy on the adult's hands. One feels, almost as if it were pictured right on the page, a faith being shaped, perhaps that no matter how unpredictable and complex a set of motions might seem, they always have their logic, their direction, and that a close attention and a filial patience will bring this logic to the surface.

Aspiring engineers refined and expressed their gift by working their way up from project to project and mentor to mentor, accumulating expertise, contacts, and reputation. A case in point was the career of John Jervis, a farm hand in his early 20s hired in the summer of 1817 as an axman by a team surveying for the Erie Canal. Over the next winter Jervis scoured the neighborhood for works on surveying, geometry, trigonometry, and navigation, and by the summer of 1818 was working on a surveying team himself. Each year thereafter he took on new responsibilities, in the discharge of which he learned to cut and blast stone and fit it with mortar, keep accounts and manage a work force, and design foundations, bridges, dams, and simple steam engines. Seven years later he was in charge of a canal project himself (the Delaware and Hudson); not many years after that his gift had made him one of the most accomplished and sought-after engineers in America. Jervis went on to design one of the standard American locomotives and the Croton reservoir (which fed New York City), among many other achievements.

By the middle of the nineteenth century these austere gentlemen had built the country's first high-tech industry and done so, having little else to work with, on the properties of water. They became masters of the design of canals, dams, reservoirs, aqueducts, sewers, river control, the drainage of marshes, fire fighting, and, above all, of hydropower, the sole branch of engineering whose domestic development could have wrung more than polite interest from a visiting European. In Europe the development of water power had been restricted from above by the assertion of manorial milling privileges, and below by attacks from guilds (like sawyers), who saw a threat to the conventional practice of their craft. Neither restraint operated in this country, which was also well watered and chronically short of labor. In every frontier community with access to a stream or brook, construction of the mill came just after the erection of personal shelter and before a general store or church. At their peak, as many as a hundred thousand mills might have been sawing lumber and grinding grain, pumping bellows for blacksmiths, powering carders and fullers (textile processes), or grinding bark for tanneries, among dozens of other uses. As industrial historian Louis Hunter has written, the basic kit of pioneering comprised four tools: the ax, the plow, the ox, and the mill.

During the nineteenth century this familiarity with moving water built the largest mills in the world, sited not on the traditional brook but on rivers hundreds of feet wide moving tens of thousands of tons of water an hour, often in flood conditions. Typically a complex would be built at a point where a river twisted 90 degrees or so; when it was finished, the river would be diverted out of its channel across the elbow into a network of supply canals, often from 50 to 80 feet wide and 10 feet deep, that carried the water to 30-foot power wheels arranged throughout the construction. (Sometimes the supply canals ran on two levels.) From these, power was bled off by revolving cables that ran to a forest of belting, connecting in turn to the individual machines. Providing the volumes of water guaranteed by contract required the mill companies to build and maintain a system of upstream reservoirs to buffer floods and droughts, construct dozens of water flow measurement wheels to collect billing information, and maintain the network of internal canals and power wheels. The entire system, from millpond to tailraces, might stretch for dozens of miles. Controlling an enterprise of such scale, complexity, and power required many innovations, not least of which was hiring an in-house staff of full-time engineers.

A complete engineer required more than craft experience and a sense for the fitness of things, however. Anyone hoping to rise in the profession needed to be able to write an unambiguous sentence; read a foreign language or two (the center of development and investment for most of these arts lay overseas); compose a blueprint; be perfectly at home with geometry and trigonometry; and possess a practitioner's command of the physics of forces and motions, the calculation of vectors, the flow of heat, and other bodies of physical knowledge. None of these were readily acquired in any very efficient way out in the field or on the shop floor. A candidate could learn much through home study, and many did, as Jervis had, but group study was also popular. An 1832 issue of *Young Mechanic* lists 17 educational societies in Boston alone, half sponsored by engineering associations like the Massachusetts Charitable Mechanics' Association or the New England Society for the Promotion of Manufactures and the Mechanic's Arts.

In 1865 yet another opened, grandly titled (considering that its first class numbered 15) "The Massachusetts Institute of Technology." A representative passage in the promotional literature promised to exchange the following services for tuition of a hundred dollars a year:

a complete course of instruction and training, suited to the various practical professions of the Mechanician, the Civil Engineer, the Builder and Architect, the Mining Engineer, and the Practical Chemist; and, at the same time, to meet the more limited aims of such as desire to secure a scientific preparation for special industrial pursuits, such as the direction of Mills, Machine Shops, Railroads, Mines, Chemical Works, Glass, Pottery and Paper manufactures, and of Dyeing, Print, and Gas works; and for the practice of Navigation and Surveying, of Telegraphy, Photography and Electrotyping, and the various other Arts having their foundation in the exact sciences.

MIT was unlike these educational societies in the breadth of its ambitions (to promote lectures, sponsor publications, maintain libraries and collections, mount exhibits, provide instruction in the scientific principles underlying all the useful arts, and organize the diffusion of scientific knowledge throughout the countryside) and in the character and qualifications of its president. William Barton Rogers had no personal experience in any of the pursuits and activities mentioned in the above paragraph, had never been any kind of engineer, did not follow a "practical occupation," had never even taught any sort of engineering, and had no prior experience in school administration, at least not in a president's office (he had chaired committees). He seems never to have even heard of the fitness of things and explicitly, even airily, dismissed craft experience as a collection of unreasoned "manipulations."

Until he took up the leadership of the new school Rogers had been known best as a geologist, specifically for research in the origins of mountains and mountain chains. Among other work he had developed a theory that these features were defined by "paroxysmal actions"—geological spasms that concentrated large changes into very short periods of time. This was by no means the settled opinion of the time; Victorian geology found the idea that an august landscape of great antiquity could be swallowed up in a morning implausible, if not indeed disturbing. However, the novelty of the perspective, as advanced by Rogers's considerable powers of presentation, had given him and his brother-colleague, Henry, national reputations.

There was much more to Rogers than geology, however. His correspondence, which was voluminous even in his day and would be torrential in this, drew freely from dozens of topics in science, engineering, politics, philosophy, and literature. While he had his personal enthusiasms—street illumination, national and local politics, the psychooptics of binocular vision, meteorology, developments in scientific instrumentation, and landscape, which his geological training allowed him to describe in depth—Rogers was able to plug his intellect into almost any subject of interest to the letter's recipient.

As various as was the subject matter, the tone of his correspondence was uniformly warm, interested, optimistic, and energetic. A picture of Rogers taken during his presidency, seated and in profile, reveals a tall, lanky gentleman so relaxed as almost to seem asleep. A rich flow of laugh lines radiates back from his eyes, disappearing into a fall of silky hair. His nose so dominates the image that an observer forced to guess the subject of the photo might imagine it an illustration of a man immersed in some delicious fragrance.

Rogers was a classic Victorian upper-middle-class liberal reformer, an enthusiastic subscriber to the idea that the species was susceptible to perpetual, continuous improvement. The attitude of the seventeenth century on the question of social change had been quite clear: that small fraction which was desirable came about through prayer and a strenuous effort to bring one's behavior into conformity with the word of God. Two hundred years later a substantial company of what Twain called the expostulating class had been won over to quite another model: that there were forces flowing through the society which, if properly harnessed, would lift each generation to a more virtuous, rational, and happier condition than that of its parents automatically, whether they had worked to that end or not.

The source of this irrepressible, self-renewing buoyancy was science, which was accepted almost everywhere in the halls of improvement as replacing holy writ in both its cultural and magical aspects. Many Victorians believed that once science had been "promulgated" to the laboring classes the incapacitating superstitions instilled by the Church and aristocracy would dissolve automatically, of their own accord. Educational reformers on both sides of the Atlantic (the most famous being Francis Owens) had been saying for years that the real agenda of traditional classical education, with its emphasis on the memorization of superfluous pedantry, was precisely to lead the mind away from the natural fruits of real education: social progress, social uplift, and social equality. Both morality and a sensible grasp of the practical realities of the time, these reformers argued, demanded the replacement of the classical model of the liberal arts with one based on fluency in the language of real life, of nature. If civilizing influences were required, a science-based education could civilize as well or better than Greek.

Rogers believed in every article of this faith. Instruction in the principles of science would not only contribute to the prosperity of the country, he once wrote; it would also lead

the thoughts of the practical student into those wide and elevated regions of reflection to which the study of Nature's laws never fails to conduct the mind. Thus linking the daily details of his profession with the grander physical agencies around him, and with much of what is agreeable and ennobling in the contemplation of external things, it would insensibly elevate and refine his character and contribute to the cheerfulness as it aided the efficiency of his labors. In this respect . . . physical studies are better capable of being useful to the operative classes than the study of literature or morals, because their truths are more readily and eagerly seized upon by such minds and form the strong staple of practical usefulness thus firmly infixed.

These sweeping lines—"the strong staple of practical usefulness thus firmly infixed!"—flowed from Rogers's pen in Charlottesville, where he was a professor of geology and natural philosophy at the University of Virginia. The university had treated Rogers well—having made him a full professor at 23—but after almost two decades on the faculty he was growing restless. As potent a force for civilization as science might be, it seems to have found its limits at the University of Virginia, which at the time was an archetypal party school. The students brought their horses and dogs from home, got drunk early and often, and even wore guns to class. Occasionally they fired a little lead pepper through the windows of faculty members whose views they found disappointing. Faculty members could of course shoot back, and apparently for many professors the opportunity of squeezing off a few rounds at their charges compensated for the danger, but Rogers was looking around.

One day in 1846 he received a letter from Henry, who was in Boston angling for a job in the geology department at Harvard, describing a chance meeting with the trustee of a will providing for the construction of a Boston technical institute of some kind. "If you and myself could be at the head of this 'Polytechnic School of the Useful Arts,'" he speculated, "it would be much pleasanter . . . for there would be less discipline, indeed, no more than with medical students." (Apparently the docility of engineers towards authority was even then general knowledge.)

Rogers immediately composed and dispatched "A Plan for a Polytechnic School in Boston" for inspection by the trustee, a Mr. Lowell. Rogers had no experience in any aspect of the "useful arts" or school management and did not know Boston. He therefore had nothing to say on the practical issues the school would face—who the polytechnic would be admitting and how, how it might raise funds, and the nature of its relations with local industry, which would be expected to hire its graduates. What he knew and believed in was science, and it was upon this point that he exerted his considerable rhetorical powers.

Rogers's plan divided useful knowledge into two categories: scientific principles and "minute details and manipulations." The first represents "physical truth," the wisdom that frees the soul and nourishes virtue; the second, reflex operations and operational trivia of the sort that could be picked up in an afternoon, like whether screws turned clockwise or counterclockwise. Summed, these categories constituted Rogers's vision of the intellectual content of the engineering.

Historically (his proposal continued) these bodies of information had been associated with two distinct and mutually isolated populations. The first, with citizens like Lavoisier and Newton and Galileo, who enjoyed a nobility of spirit and freedom of intellect that allowed them to survey nature as from a great height. These worthies grasped the "basis" of natural phenomena and from that perspective were able to add to society's store of "physical truth." The second, with the operatives or industrial classes: builders, "practical chemists," engineers, manufacturers, and mechanics, who stumbled along from generation to generation recycling rules of thumb with no greater base in natural logic than the belief of twelfth-century blacksmiths that metals were best quenched in the urine of 12-year-old red-headed boys.

These groups spent no very great time in each other's company. Occasionally a scrap of physical truth would fall from the head table, as when Benjamin Franklin had been gracious enough to interest himself in practical affairs. When that happened, and usually *only* when that happened, society advanced. "the unexampled progress," Rogers wrote, "both here and in Europe, of every branch of the arts for the last 50 years is but the result of that general diffusion of a better knowledge of physical laws which has flowed from the researches and teachings of men specially devoted to natural science . . . " What was required was a formal, institutionalized link between science and society, between scientists and the citizenry in general. The institute envisaged in Rogers's proposal was to be this link.

Lowell ended up giving the money to Harvard, perhaps because he found Rogers's proposal weak on details, perhaps because the fix was in in any case. He did, however, circulate the draft, and over the next few years it gradually developed an audience. In this context, passing from hand to hand, audience to audience, the lack of detail proved a strength: the plan stuck to one central point on which everyone agreed, the importance of science in the coming age. Each group looked to science to cure a different disease: liberal reformers thought it would pry religion off the windpipe of the culture; manufacturers, that training in science would be a cheap way to increase the pool of skilled labor and lower its cost; merchants and civic boosters, that it would bring prosperity and international stature to the region; operatives and engineers, that a reputation for scientific training might win them the social standing of lawyers and doctors, if not that of preachers.

A correspondence sprang up between Boston and Charlottesville, and within a few years interest had grown (and the climate in Virginia had deteriorated; while no radical, Rogers was distinctly abolitionist in his sympathies) sufficiently to encourage Rogers to move North to direct affairs personally. He turned out to have a rare talent for politics, or at least for Boston politics, combining energy, flexible sympathies and interests, charm, clarity of goal, a fluent command of rhetorical gesture, and a personal sincerity so luminous it placed his own motives above inquiry, let alone question. Once, when some issue in which Rogers was interested was scheduled for hearings before the legislature, the governor of Massachusetts wrote Rogers to advise that, contrary to the usual custom of politics, it would be best for his testimony to go unsupported. Rogers's devotion to the public weal was unquestioned, the savvy worthy explained, but anyone else speaking in favor of the question might be suspected of private purposes, and that suspicion could diminish the political effect of Rogers's testimony.

This reputation gave the reformer extraordinary authority and privilege. For example, to skip ahead a few years, in 1862 the federal government passed an act supporting public education with funds raised through the sale of public lands. (About $100,000 was at stake, the equivalent of $20 million today.) Up till that point in the history of the state all such goodies had been forwarded to Harvard College as a matter of course. This time, when Harvard announced its willingness to legitimize the Morrill Act by accepting its money, the money was gone: Rogers had whisked it off, in the interest of a school that then existed only on paper.

In the late 1850s a proposal was introduced into the Massachusetts legislature to set some public lands in Boston aside for educational purposes. A coalition of reformers and public institutions, Rogers among them, sailed into the legislature after the property, only to be unhorsed by some last-minute private dealing. The year after Rogers organized a narrower application for the property, one focused entirely on a "school of industrial science"; he developed groups of boosters in every senate district in the state. This time he won. The same political skill coaxed construction money from various merchants. When the school opened in 1865 Rogers was the inevitable choice for president.

Most of MIT's students were men of age and acquirements: contractors, "operatives," supervisors of works, artisan-mechanics, apprentices, and journeyman engineers, who registered for small numbers of courses in specialized subjects, like mechanical drawing or mining machinery, for which they had specific ends in view. There was no campus life: no dormitories (the students either commuted for the duration of their courses or rented a room in a local boarding house); no chapel (in an age when most educational institutions insisted on attendance for at least Sunday services); and, until 1876, not even a lunch room. A later president limned the distinction incisively when he wrote, "This is a place for men to work, not for boys to play" (words that echo down the corridors of the Institute to this day).

Right from the first year, however, Rogers admitted in addition to these skilled practitioners utter novices, teenaged boys (the first teenaged girls arrived in the 1870s) of no experience who stayed for two (later four) years and upon graduation were handed a degree in engineering science. From the point of view of attracting employment they would have found more utility in a new suit or a watch. Academic undergraduate engineering education was less a new idea than a failed one: In 1824 Rensselaer Polytechnic had been founded in Troy, New York, as part of a utopian experiment, and most of the major colleges offered engineering majors. But Rensselaer had never attracted more than a handful of students, and engineering majors were widely regarded as nothing but convenient devices for extracting tuition from those intellectually unable to endure the years of Latin, Greek, and Hebrew required in serious fields of study, like divinity or literature. There were also some European technical schools, like the Polytechnic Institute of Karlsruhe, but few employers would have heard of them, let alone thought through the applicability of their example to local conditions.

The professional prejudice against academic engineering education was straightforward and commonsensical. Academies admitted on the basis of paper tests, patently a poor filter for a quick and open eye and a sense for natural practicalities, let alone for the gift. That they awarded passing grades of 70 percent, or even 60 percent, was a fatal self-indictment. ("Engineering is a 100 percent profession," these critics liked to point out.) Since successful practitioners would have no reason to retire from real life to the must of academia, most of these institutions were and would continue to be staffed by failures, professional educators who would have taught anything whatever— literature, deportment, ballroom dancing—for the prospect of a pension.

Just as crippling were the pretensions inherent to academic culture. What little practical experience students were exposed to, and that was little indeed, came from "demonstrations" in a school "laboratory." Heaven forfend that they should "work" in a "shop." As one engineer wrote, in his experience professors of engineering "looked on manual training as the preceptress in a young ladies' seminary might instruction in laundry work . . . not to make washer-women of [her pupils], but that they might know [enough to criticize without] being laughed at." The value of shop culture, of the thought and experience of the workmen, the real operatives, was belittled at every turn. How could a man turn up his nose at this source of practical authority and succeed? Frederick Winslow Taylor, inventor of time and motion studies and not one to be loose with a number, estimated that a year in a machine shop was worth 20 in school.

But the fundamental problem was that the skills academia taught comprised about 5 percent of the business. An engineer in those days had to be prepared to look for "the fitness of things" in a tremendous range of subjects: the same person had to negotiate some realism into the grandiose schemes promoters used to entice investors, draw up a design that was sensitive to the range and quality of parts and labor locally available, decode the descriptions in catalogues for those that were not, plan the sequence of orders, supervise the construction of parts (often, machines to make machines), define tests to catch the flaws in the parts, and monitor expenses, all the time handling investor relations, supplier negotiations, personnel management, contractor supervision, and the needs of the local political structure. What school could possibly teach any of these subjects, let alone the art of their trade-offs? From the point of view of the elite, calling someone an engineer who had learnt engineering from books made as much sense as hiring a cook who had learnt food preparation from pictures, or going whaling with a group of librarians fresh from a deep read of *Moby Dick*. Tuition extracted under such pretenses was little better than fraud.

What could seem more plausible? It was, however, a line of argument for which Rogers, with his faith in the elevating powers of science and lack of first-hand experience in engineering itself, made a poor audience. He continued to accept raw youths, stuff them with the scriptures of Newton, Boyle, Ohm, Carnot, Joule, and Helmholtz and send them out into the world. On the evidence of the first class reports, the "regular" graduates of MIT, as this minority of younger, full-time, students were called, had a hard time. Some taught; others went West; a small but constant fraction became landscape painters (Tech was strong on drawing and drafting). More than a few ended up in sales.

After the first decade, however, the climate seems to have warmed. During the 1880s, the expansion of the electrical and chemical industries, neither with any pool of conventionally trained labor to draw on, screwed the demand for technically skilled labor from the intense to the desperate, and employers began to change their standards. MIT graduates might be all theory, but they were cheap and eager and at least they knew the names of materials, the physical constants, the conversion factors, the basic formulas. Slowly manufacturers began to take on new hires with degrees, fresh out of school. Against the general expectation, they found the results encouraging enough to continue.

Once it became clear that the academically trained engineer was employable, the apprentice and mentor system was doomed. Under the old regime, a young person who couldn't find the right kind of job at the right time risked not only wages but a future in the profession. Academic education might be impractical in some respects, but every fall the school admitted a class and four years later awarded its members a piece of paper welcoming them into the collectivity of white collars. To a young person eager to get on with life this was the essence of practicality.

From the perspective of society at large the advantage of academic education was that it could be expanded quickly and almost without limit. In the old system an industrialist wishing to add to his payroll was dependent on the recent history of his industry; if it had been depressed, or was new, as in electrical equipment, the workforce was just not there. Scaling in an academy was a simple matter of hiring another professor and renting a classroom; multiplying academies themselves took little more effort than writing out a charter. Over the last third of the nineteenth century more than a hundred schools of engineering opened their doors, and by 1900 classroom-based engineering education had become the normal road of entry to the field. In short, as implausible as it might have looked, academic engineering education worked. Some factor invisible to the old guard had entered the game. Perhaps a sense for the fitness of things was more common than the masters had thought. Perhaps the nature of engineering had changed.

Toward the end of the 1900s certain keen observers, Henry Adams preeminently among them, pointed out that the pace of technological change had become exponential. "Evidently a new variety of mind had appeared," Adams wrote. "Certain men merely held out their hands—like Newton, watched an apple; like Franklin, flew a kite; like Watt, played with a tea kettle—and great forces of nature stuck to them as though she were playing ball." Adams did not develop this idea of a "new mind," but it is worth pursuing.

During the eighteenth and nineteenth centuries the various natural philosophers had gradually hammered out a language unlike any heard on the globe to that date, one in which each word had only one meaning and the meanings of no two words overlapped. Applied to nature this language yielded exact, standard, definitions of basic units like time and temperature and of natural phenomena like rocks and species and substances. The peculiar virtue of this language was that it allowed those divided by barriers that might ordinarily have inhibited communication both to understand each other and to know they were being understood. The unambiguous precision of these terms allowed minds separated by space and time, by generation and culture, by class and character and philosophy, to focus on the same subject matter and explore its nature and relations communally. As the mails improved and the scientific press grew in breadth and circulation, hundreds and then thousands of minds plugged into the conversation.

If Adams was right in thinking that a "new kind of mind had appeared," he was wrong to guess these minds belonged to individuals. What had appeared was a group mind of a scale no tribe or clan had ever enjoyed, one with extraordinary powers of penetration, comprehension, clarification, and curiosity. As scientific societies spread, this new instrument for channeling and coordinating the intelligence of civilization became fabulously productive. No other organ of culture—politics, religion, art—developed anything comparable. Little wonder science went in a hundred years from little more than the hobby of a handful of bright curates and leisured aristos to the most dynamic and prestigious activity of the culture.

Science used this language as a tool for analysis, defining the lines along which phenomena were to be divided, but it was as good an instrument for synthesis, for carrying communication about the integration of geometries, properties, and processes. Even pups from engineering schools could use it to compensate for their ignorance with the forces of community. Perhaps the average product of academic engineering education was inferior to the minds and spirits that constituted the profession throughout much of the nineteenth century, but they had the language. Perhaps that power made the difference.

Rogers thought of himself as a scientist, not an "operative." In retrospect, however, he emerges as a metaengineer, a designer of processes that turned a field composed by a small if impressive elite into the second largest profession in the country (after education), with a membership of 1 percent of the population. (Which, not so incidentally, lowered the unit cost of engineering drastically.) Inadvertently, perhaps, he found a new quality of fitness—fittingness—in human communication, a quality that opened the doors to solution space, allowing millions to join the circulation of connections.

FOUR

The Architecture of Solution Space

By the turn of the century the rising tide of Boston development had begun to price MIT out of its address in Copley Square. (Ironically so, given the role of the thousands of engineers graduated since 1865 in driving those tides.) Lab by lab, bits of the Institute scattered out into the greater Boston real estate market, hunting for rents more appropriate to an organization that had just begun to meet its payroll with any consistency. The stick of watching MIT disintegrate, together with the carrot of cashing out at the top of the market, brought all parties to the conclusion that Tech had to move. The last piece fell in place in 1909, when MIT discovered in its new president, Richard Maclaurin, the first effective fund-raiser since William Rogers. Maclaurin worked the Du Ponts and the Lowells and stroked George

Eastman; in short order he had the wherewithal to gather these fragments to a single address.

One candidate was a landfill then being extended from the Cambridge bank of the Charles, a river running between that city and Boston. To the site's disadvantage, the art of building large structures on river landfill was not cut-and-dried: the soil was wet and new, and would certainly settle under heavy construction. On the other hand, the institutional politics were extremely auspicious. Just the rumor that MIT was thinking of moving to Cambridge had forced a most satisfying letter out of the office of the president of Harvard. The fraction of real estate the taxpayers of Cambridge would be willing to see disappear from the tax rolls must be expected to have a bottom, Lowell had pointed out, and surely everyone could agree that that bottom belonged to Harvard. Relocating across the Charles, to Harvard's side of the river, while perhaps not technically squatting or poaching, could conceivably throw some future expansion of The University into question. If the consequent risks were hard to estimate, surely no responsible citizen would wish to provoke them while alternatives existed.

Harvard and its arrogance were topics that kept MIT alumni, especially those working around Boston, in a state of chronic dyspepsia. (Maclaurin's predecessor, Henry Pritchett, lost his job in large part by endorsing the swap of a titular unification with that university for a massive endowment.) The belief that participation in the world of artifacts was intellectually and spiritually inferior to participation in the world of nature, including the world of the poetic imagination, ran right to the root of the literary culture that was Harvard's clock and compass. "This country is a constant whirl of dollars and railroads and commerce and invention," a distinguished Boston elder wrote to urge a nephew considering a position on the MIT faculty to teach at Harvard instead. "Every city is capable of a common school, or High School, or School of Arts and Metiers [the elder's term for MIT]; but it is only at such a place as Cambridge [i.e., Harvard], with its atmosphere of learning and its learned memories, that we may hope for a *University*: a place where the grander harmonies of the Universe may be studied."

One thread devaluing tool making might have been spun from the aristocratic disdain for "trade"; a second, out of the theological point that natural objects come from God and artifacts, from the stained and corrupt hand of man. Whatever, the literary culture saw no need to extend to the members of this new profession the social prerogatives granted as a matter of course to lawyers and scientists and college professors. During the 1890s one of the two professors Harvard then retained to teach "applied" subjects was asked what life on the faculty was like. The social obligations will drive you to bankruptcy, the professor said, but they are not the worst, pulling out a letter from the dean that had arrived that very day. Apparently some Dartmouth youths had visited the campus, for the statue of John Harvard had turned green and the maintenance staff was having trouble removing the paint. Would it be possible for the professor to nip over and use his command of the applied arts to help them out? I get these all the time, he said. When his visitor, an MIT graduate, recorded this incident in his memoirs 30 years later, he did so more in amusement than indignation, as a perfectly representative instance of the rain of professional denigration to which Tech graduates were routinely subjected by Boston society.

To working engineers this assumption of cultural inferiority was naturally infuriating, not least because from their

perspective science and engineering were simple recipro-
cals; any statement you might make about the intellectual or
spiritual content of one applied equally, if in inverted form,
to the other. Engineering could be seen as a special case of
science ("applied science"), but science could equally well
be described as a special case of engineering ("abstract
engineering"); what was science but the design of the conceptual tools required to gain access to the natural order?
Scientists are given a phenomenon and asked to find its
logical and physical relations to the rest of the universe;
engineers are given the relations and asked to define the
phenomenon. (Scientists derive the specifications from the
object; engineers, the object from the specifications.) Studying an artifact in order to figure out its logic is known as
"reverse engineering"; in that usage science is the reverse
engineering of nature and engineering the science of solution space. Each design is an experimental hypothesis.*
Science is understanding where you are; engineering is
getting there. How can one half of this cycle be set against
the other?

Even when the symmetry breaks down it is not clear it
does so to the disadvantage of engineering. An advocate
might argue that only through engineering is it possible to
have more than the most glancing and episodic relationship
with the "grander harmonies": scientists observe nature
from outside, while engineers and nature get married and
have progeny. They build day-in, day-out, working relation-
ships out of common interests and shared goals. Surely the
fitness of things, the power of connectedness that runs
through the universe of mind and matter alike, is as grand
and sanctified a harmony as the taxonomy of butterflies or

---

*Francis Bacon wrote that "human knowledge and human power meet in one;
for . . . that which in contemplation is as the cause is in operation as the rule."

the geography of the ocean bottom. If humans are as much a part of nature as rainbows, then it is hard to see why their tools should be any more artificial than the colors refracted from raindrops. Similarly, if the universe was made by God, what makes nature less artifactual than bricks or glass? ("All things are artificial," Thomas Browne wrote, "for Nature is the art of God.")

In short, almost all Tech graduates felt the prejudice of the literary community, thought it groundless and arbitrary, and were intensely sensitive to the assumption pervading the tribe of inbred longnoses that they were so many batboys to be ordered about at whim. Moving to Cambridge, especially in the face of an explicit request to go elsewhere, was symbolically elbowing in at the head of the table.

A s attractive as the politics might be, the issue of the structural integrity of the soil remained a potential headache, so early on in the process Maclaurin arranged a conference with a hydraulics engineer who had been involved with several large engineering projects on the Charles. Though a graduate of the Institute himself, John Ripley Freeman was cut from the cloth of one of the old masters, a man whose sense for the fitness of things embraced every topic he met. He was an expert on hydropower; the author of a series of influential research papers on fire pumps, hose, sprinklers, and hydrants; the inventor of a widely used sprinkler head; director of a flourishing private practice (including a consultancy on the Panama Canal and a stint as advisor to the Chinese government on river flooding); and president of the largest industrial fire insurance company in America. Freeman was also fiercely devoted to MIT: secretary of his class, president of the alumni association, one-time member of the corporation, a staunch advocate of establishing science as the basis of a new liberal arts, and perfectly willing to use his corporate position ("against much opposition," he once wrote) to hire MIT graduates into his firm.

At one point Freeman was even sounded for his interest in the presidency of MIT. According to legend, he shrugged these feelers off with the remark that he was "not much in the dinner-jacket line." This apparently unmemorable comment has entered the canon of mainline MIT historiography; whenever Institute documents refer to the hydraulicist the story bobs to the surface. However the remark was meant, it has been taken as an affirmation of the values of the profession: Real engineers do not schmooze. Over time usage has transformed this throwaway line to an affectionate tribute, like an epitaph: "John Ripley Freeman: Not Much in the Dinner-Jacket Line." Surviving photos of Freeman show a small man, thin, with neat features, a Vandyke beard, and a habit of leaning forward on the balls of his feet, as though about to bounce. In group photos he seems to strain to lift off, like a slim balloon in a suit. For what it might be worth, on the testimony of these photos Freeman was a bit of a fop: at least he usually seems to be wearing the suit with the most intricate cut and the most natural and unwrinkled drape.

Freeman certified the load-bearing capacities of the Cambridge site and announced himself delighted with the plan; so delighted, he told Maclaurin, that he entertained the hope of being named architect for the entire complex. University presidents earn, or fail to earn, their salary at such moments. On the one hand, no university president could possibly have handed over the millions Maclaurin had raised to a man whose major design triumph to date had been a sprinkler head, as excellent as that head might have been; on the other, MIT had a bare handful of alumni of comparable status, and even fewer as devoted to the institution, especially as regarded the hiring of its graduates. No doubt, as presidents do, Maclaurin carefully expressed a deep interest in Freeman's extremely provocative and stimulating proposal and promised to take it under the most active advisement. And perhaps the engineer was not in fact perfectly adapted to the subtleties of the dinner-jacket world, since at the end of the conversation he steamed away thinking he had Maclaurin's blessing.

In time the finished design arrived in the president's office, accompanied by a text that presented the design as the opening salvo of a cultural revolution. Higher education, Freeman wrote, had been abducted by "the motive of monumentality"—the practice of designing not buildings but monuments to the benefactor's generosity, backdrops for dedication ceremonies, stage sets. Over and over, issues involving the conduct of the actual work, like adequate office and classroom space, lighting, and sensible traffic patterns had been subordinated to professional self-promotion and obscurantist mumbo jumbo. Such priorities were not just out of place—they were outrageous, and yet they were everywhere.

The agents of this corruption, Freeman continued, were architects, an airy bunch of actors, Harvard graduates mostly, who measured their professional competence by the degree to which their designs reflected obsequiousness toward wealth and contempt for honest function. If the productive enterprises of America had had to depend on architects for shelter, one infers, they would today lie naked to the weather. Fortunately, there was a second category of professional designing structures for organizations: industrial engineers (sometimes called mill architects). Industrial engineers designed mills, factories, warehouses, field offices, loading docks, and piers: structures that did more than sit and bat their eyes at old money.

These men gave an honest day's work and respected the desire of others to do the same. They brought their projects in on time and to budget—both acts that architects, judging from their behavior, believed would cost their professional license. They were not above giving details like ventilation, maintenance, fire prevention, and intelligent traffic flow priority over the play of Tudor-Gothic harmonies. They systematically resolved all design issues so as to support the activities internal to the building, as opposed to publicizing the creative powers of the artist, elevating the stature of the donor, or indulging the aesthetic satisfaction of tourists.

For one example, industrial engineers had pioneered the use of modular elements—defining a single basic door, window, or staircase that worked in every region or corner of the structure. This freed contractors from buying small lots of hand-made elements, permitting handsome savings. Mill engineers had also learned how to use walkways and causeways and tunnels to promote social interaction. In production or distribution sites of even moderate complexity, streams of clerks, operators, inspectors, superintendents, technicians, mechanics, parts and services salespeople, and process and maintenance engineers were continually moving and mixing. Manufacturing structures had to allow people to pick up and visit each other anywhere in the complex, day or night, perhaps wheeling a cart or dolly laden with equipment, without having to think about the weather or the terrain or even whether to wear a coat. To Freeman it seemed obvious that these grids of broad, open, uncluttered, protected corridors, which he thought ideal for cultivating the social and cooperative instincts, were appropriate for a college; for any college, not just a technical school, but certainly for a school like MIT.

Yet when we tour an American campus, Freeman wrote, what do we see?

Buildings of widely different architectural types scattered over a campus, [with] each department, so far as possible, isolated and housed in a separate building so that the professor in charge . . . reigns undisturbed, in a little kingdom of his own, [while] the undergraduate student . . . spends some valuable time and runs much risk of colds in our northern climate, in passing from one lecture to another, and in many cases must hurry so . . . that all opportunity for personal contact with the lecturer is lost.

"True, he gets the benefit of filling his lungs with fresh air," Freeman continued sarcastically, "which becomes of greater importance by reason of the wretched ventilation that commonly prevails in college lecture rooms and laboratories, but the process or lack of arrangement involves a waste that could hardly be tolerated in commercial life."

In sum, while architects had been strutting about on center stage flaunting their *motifs*, industrial engineers had been accumulating serious experience in, and doing some real engineering about, the interaction of people and tasks with structures. This progress was a fruit ready for harvesting, "an opportunity for a vast improvement in the efficiency of college architecture," and the new MIT campus was a natural place for its debut. "Architectural" considerations would not go entirely without a role, but for the most part, Freeman believed, the design of the Institute should be drawn from the experience and reflect the values of people who knew how to make a building work for a living. If it were, the campus would work, come in under budget, present a compelling advertisement for the values of the

Institute, and show universities everywhere the path to freedom from the fanciful vanities of architectural design.

No one looking at the drawing accompanying Freeman's plan, which in its larger features resembles an enormous length of duct pipe bent in a U-shape, would for a moment doubt his contempt for functionless aesthetics. (Though Freeman never makes the analogy, the corridors seem to quote, thematically, from the network of supply canals and millraces that fed the hydropower mills of the nineteenth century.) The design is uncompromisingly, even magnificently, ugly, a fist in the nose of traditional campus architecture. Freeman even planned to face the buildings with concrete instead of crushed limestone. We are more tolerant of this material today, but by the standards of the time concrete was a barbarism. No building had yet been faced in it, though it was mechanically adequate and comparatively cheap.

No doubt the building would have made a revolutionary break with the architectural conventions of the time; perhaps that break would have swept the architects into the sea. If the revolution failed, however, the Institute would have been hip-deep in ridicule. Maclaurin's fund-raising had been defined around the idea that MIT was a national school with a national mission; the last thing he needed was an identification with idiosyncrasy. He thanked Freeman for his valuable time and constructive thinking and went out and hired one Welles Bosworth, a professional much favored by the upper crust—John D. Rockefeller was a client—as the architect of record for the new complex.

Freeman took Maclaurin's hiring of the foremost practitioner of the very aesthetic he found so destructive and contemptible as a personal repudiation. After (uncharacteristically) circulating dark speculations about the nature of Bosworth's influence with Mrs. Maclaurin, he cut his relations with MIT altogether. Even a quarter century later, when he wrote his memoirs, he could not bring himself to mention a word of this episode, or indeed anything of his extensive alumni relations with the Institute.

If Freeman was surprised by the behavior of the man he had counted on as a friend and ally he must have been astounded by that of the man he had thought his enemy. Bosworth read Freeman's design, the denunciations of his profession included, and was intrigued by it. (It is possible that the architect's enormously acute professional antennae were even then picking up the first tremors of the revolution that was to sweep the world of design a decade later, in which ideas like defining form from function, designing from standard units, and generally following the inspiration of industrial designers were to make international stars out of Walter Gropius and the other architects of the Bauhaus.) Bosworth added an open grassy court facing south over the Charles, a large Greek temple dome, and replaced the exterior concrete with the traditional crushed limestone. But he kept the guts of Freeman's design: the huge interconnecting corridors and the modular elements, so that what one sees from the inside is very close to the original. The final bill was way over budget, of course, but Bosworth had given Maclaurin a picture he could raise money with. MIT moved to its new campus in 1916.

Nothing since has questioned the wisdom of these decisions. The soil has supported the campus; the matrix has proved its worth as the natural architecture of solution space; and MIT is a co-equal player with Harvard in every field on which the two meet, including presumptive rights to the last certificate of tax exemption to be squeezed out of the City of Cambridge. The tensions at play between the institutions have by no means disappeared, however. "The fastest way to kill an idea around here is to identify it with Harvard," a dean once told me. "We have a lot of differences on what we want to be or do, but we know we don't want to be *that*." And on the other side, often enough the literary sensibility still believes that engineering does not have quite the same standing, make the same claim on the intelligence, as the study of the grander harmonies. When journalists write stories about some technological development they often do the engineers developing the device the favor of calling them "scientists," presumably to add a little gravity to the story. (From *The Wall Street Journal*: "NEENAH, Wis.—Inside an old Ford dealer's garage here, Kimberly-Clark Corp. scientists quietly worked on a top secret project called Omega. They envisaged disposable training pants, a cross between absorbable diapers and underwear . . .")

The products of engineering are tools, and the test of a well-made tool, of one that is a credit to its designer, is the speed with which it vanishes into the consciousness of its user. (This is what distinguishes tool making from sculpture.) When we fly to some city we say that "we" flew there, not that the jet did; while it might be technically inaccurate to say that "guns don't kill people, people do," no gun company would wish to market a product that left the opposite impression. Literary, artistic creations have their moments of independence, when they are exhibited or bought or published, but the connection to creator is never finally severed, if only because the object retains a quality of separate existence. This is less true of scientific contributions but not drastically so: natural phenomena are plastered with the names of their discoverers— Einsteinian relativity, Darwinian selection, Newton's laws, Young's modulus, Rayleigh scattering, Maxwell's equations, Planck's constant, the Bohr radius, and so on.

Nobody knows or cares to know the names of those responsible for designing the tools they use at work and home, unless the designer happened to go on to make a fortune, like Bill Gates of Microsoft. It could be no other way, if only because tools are never really designed, in the sense of finished. Every specific example is in flux, contingent, partially undone. An art object, once made, can stand forever in that form; in theory, it might stir feelings as long as the species survives. A piece of science, if true, can explain the phenomena it addresses (to the same degree of precision) forever. By contrast, every design balances—connects—dozens of values, like a conceptual mobile, and the weights of those values, their relative utility or attractiveness, are changing constantly. (Often the very invention of the device changes the weights.) "At some point in every project," managers like to say, "you have to shoot the engineers and ship." But of course that just changes the address at which the tinkering is done; the thread is picked up in other companies, by other generations and other cultures. Finally, from the point of view of the profession, the measure of a truly great design is success in contexts entirely unimagined by its innovator, like the airplane or the personal computer. A great design *attracts* applications, and in doing so necessarily makes its creator look short-sighted and slightly dumb. To a young person hungry for the acclaim of the world, for honors and reputation, this must seem the most problematical of careers.

MIT has grown considerably since 1916, but that growth has been guided by Freeman's original principles. With a few exceptions, the buildings that have gone up since have been woven into the net of corridors. The new buildings have tended to be long, low (around five stories high), and thin, so that from a distance it seems as though the corridors had swallowed a series of large boxes. The campus still has its raw edge, aesthetically speaking. From time to time MIT commissions a sculpture by a distinguished artist—there is a Calder here, a Moore, a Nevelson, a Picasso—but most seem as out of place as if they had fallen off a truck. (Except for the Calder, a wonderfully whimsical concatenation of parabolic curves held together by conspicuous trails of rivets, suggesting that even those most abstract of constructions, mathematical formulae, are at bottom only bits of engineering.) The Nevelson is a nervous flurry of flanges and arms running off every whichway, expressing the self-conscious discomfort of a person lost in a neighborhood in which he has no business and knows the inhabitants know it.

A visitor—a nervous 17-year-old, a CEO from Boise, an industrial spy, a tourist from Singapore—accustomed to the look and traffic patterns of major universities might find the grounds of the MIT campus remarkably underpopulated. Responsible people can speedskate over the sidewalks and do. In the spring and summer, when the sails of the Lasers and Mercuries and Mistral windsurfers flutter against the brick backdrop of the Boston cityscape, the vista from Killian Court in particular has no local peer for elegance. Yet aside from occasions like fetes for the alumni, it is usually virtually deserted.

The real campus, the heart, is Freeman's matrix. Everything outside these walls is so much periphery. Twice a year the sun sets such that for a few moments its rays run parallel to the walls of the corridor; these days have become the subject of a low-key semi-annual celebration. A few minutes before the instant of perfectly parallel alignment, students and staffers gather along the walls, sighting up the broad strip of gold being poured by the sun over the Indiana limestone from which the floors of the corridor were built.

There is no way to see when the moment arrives: the change of the angle of ray to wall is too subtle. It must be calculated, but of course it is, and at exactly the right moment the conversations die out as if a command had been given. I have seen some participants, celebrants, reach into the corridor as if to shake hands with the rays as they fly by. What is being marked is not the simple fact of the sun shining down some hallway, since at this latitude the points at which the sun sets over the year embrace more than a quarter of the horizon. What seems to touch the spirit is the thought of the sun penetrating the matrix, plunging down into the corridors, following the general action of the house.

The first act of citizenship of a new member of the community is to find a map and internalize—"memorize" is too weak a term—the matrix. Institute folklore has it that an alert eye can sometimes pick out pencil lines on the corridor walls, shoulder high and parallel to the floor. These are supposed to be the spoor of members of the community so adapted to the corridors that they can navigate them blind: to get to point X, they filter the requisite pattern of right and left turns from an internal map, press a pencil against the wall, roll their eyeballs up into their heads, go out-of-body after some complex problem, and wheel away on automatic pilot. Whenever the pencil bounces off the wall, some semiconscious process running in their medulla oblongata scans the directions list and sends the appropriate signals to the legs.

Once they know the map advanced students graduate to the undocumented network, the corridors behind the walls: steam tunnels, ventilation ducts, maintenance passageways. Even the most remote and inaccessible corners—especially the most inaccessible corners—are crusted with initials and pseudonyms, built up over decades. The elevator shafts carry an impasto of logos (Equinox, Chance) and the occasional poem:

Invisible airwaves
Crackle with life;
Bright antennae
Bristle with energy.

grading up into the shadows as high as a flashlight beam can reach. Once a student walked me through this alternative roadway, under the bowels of the heating plant, up over the roof, in and out of the storage vaults. In theory he was my guide, but in fact I felt as if I were tagging along on an established patrol. "I like the corridors," he said, stopping and seeming to sniff them. "They never change." Once he had penetrated a building on a particularly remote part of the campus, surfed the elevator (rode on it, not in it) to a crawlway just under the roof of the building, and ducked in. It seemed like virgin territory—there were no logos painted anywhere—but at the far end of the crawlway the student found a 1958 course catalog leaning against the wall. A bullet hole had been drilled right through its center. Decades ago another student had arranged this work of MIT art, confident that sooner or later his audience would appear out of the corridors, and that for that audience nothing would have changed.

FIVE

Engineering Science

A scholar leafing through the speeches of MIT's presidents would find every reason to think Rogers's successors had faithfully tended his vision of a science-centered curriculum. Retiring presidents always review with pride their success at restoring science to its proper eminence, and new ones never fail to declare their intention of reestablishing the Institute on the ideals of its patriarch. Nonetheless, the photos of the first three quarter-centuries of Institute history suggest a slightly different story, showing room after room of big, heavy, powerful machines clearly more industrial in scale and design than would be necessary to teach the laws and constants of science.

For the first half of the century MIT graduates were not expected to be inventors or innovators (though of course many were), but tweakers, incrementalists, who worked to move the productivity of industry's capital goods one or two percentage points a year. They might be asked to redesign an 80-line telephone relay switch so it could handle 160 calls (and then 320, and then 640, etc.), or to expand the range of wattages available in light bulbs from four models to six, or to move the horsepower of an internal combustion engine one class higher. For most of its first century an astrologer would have described MIT as a Capricorn culture, a place that scaled its mountains one step at a time. In terms of curriculum, this meant spending several hours a week exploring in detail the operation of machines representative of those in use in industry. The student would adjust the machine to reflect one set of operating conditions, record the effect on performance measured in the lab notebook, then move it to another setting, and so on, until both the theory and the actual performance curves were scored deep into his or her brain stem.

No doubt this style of education had its moments of tedium, but some alumni remember it with warmth. The high cost of introducing radical modifications into such large machines meant that lab exercises hardly varied from year to year, which gave those browsing the files compiled by the MIT fraternities a sure feel for the questions likely to be asked during a term for any course. On a less practical level, imagine the reaction of a new student, fresh from a boyhood spent building bird houses, taking apart clocks, sculpting papier-mâché model railroad landscapes, assembling and disassembling lawnmowers and bicycles, walking through the door to the Dynamo Lab of the electrical engineering department.

This was a large room, 80 feet long and 20 high, with great round metal structures the size of small cars—motors, generators, transformers—sitting on spring-loaded pallets or beds of jacks designed to prevent their vibrations from tearing up the floor. A 10-ton crane with an enclosed cab hung from the ceiling, and loops and twists of inch-thick cables and power jacks the size of belaying pins and arrays of circuit breakers ran along the walls. The equipment dollies were big as golf carts. The ozone in the air suggested enough electrical power to fry an entire high school like a strip of bacon. "If this wasn't engineering," an alumnus told me, the memory glowing deep in his eyes, "then engineering didn't exist." The students in photos of the Lab wear quiet ties in block colors, white shirts, and charcoal wool suits. Many wear vests. Nineteen or twenty years old, they must be, but they carry themselves as soberly and confidently as the head of a household of six. No doubt these photos are far from candid—nobody would have worn a suit routinely around these machines—but the gravity, the sobriety, seems credible enough: these were grown-up machines, and being a grown-up was part of the magic needed to run them.

This style of education tied the student directly into the real world, into real companies and real jobs. Its necessary corollary was a certain impatience with the ruminations of theorists, i.e., scientists. Prewar MIT taught science, but not much of it. Until the 1930s the sciences had not even won the most elementary of political battles in academia: their own departmental structure. Until then, any physicist employed at MIT worked for one of the engineering departments, period. Richard Feynman, an undergraduate at MIT in these years, remembers he startled one of his physics professors by declaring an intention to pursue graduate studies at the Institute.

"Why?" the professor asked.

"Because MIT is the best school for science in the country!" Feynman said loyally.

"You think that?" the professor said.

"Yeah."

"That's why you should go to some other school," the professor replied.

In 1940 the U.S. military set up a project on campus to look into a British invention called radar. This was in no sense an MIT initiative; there was no natural connection between radar and any other activity on campus (no radar industry requiring tweaking, because none existed). The president of the Institute, Karl Compton, was initially skeptical about getting involved at all. The military's interest was purely geographical: Radar was seen as a tool for coastal defense, and the New England coastline offered a full plate of coastal geometries and potential targets. MIT had a railroad siding and enough experience in managing research projects (compared with the alternatives in the Boston area, which from the military perspective were so many theological schools and art academies) to be trusted to handle the payroll and run the cafeteria. For the actual scientific direction of the project the government brought in a real scientist: Lee Du-Bridge from the University of Rochester.

Within a year Pearl Harbor had given the military the resources needed to explore every aspect of this exciting new weapon, and 200,000 square feet of lab space rose on the north edge of the campus. The building enclosing this space was called the Radiation Lab, or Rad Lab, with the intention of misdirecting the forces of Nazi espionage, since at the time "radiation" had no connotations of military interest. Strangely, no attempt at subterfuge was made with the architecture. Built along the lines of a rambling, three-story, Georgia barracks, though out of cinder block and asbestos tile instead of #3 knotty pine, Building 20 shouts its military provenance. Perhaps the design helped the community—which naturally got mass deferments from the draft—feel like part of the war effort; certainly the project itself, with its enormous local payroll, military associations, fascinating technical issues, and urgent atmosphere, became the axis around which the campus revolved.

While radars can be built to work at any frequency that penetrates air and reflects off surfaces, the interests of the military grew exponentially the farther "up" the electromagnetic spectrum (the shorter the wavelength or the higher the frequency) it looked. The radars of the time could not distinguish fighters from bombers, or detect headings, or the number of planes in a flight. Since shorter wavelengths gave finer levels of resolution (they constitute a smaller measuring stick), they would bring all these ends within reach. Shorter wavelengths also permitted smaller antennas, allowing working models to be fitted into airplanes, and this was a very high priority.

The properties of electromagnetic radiation vary enormously with wavelength. In one part of the spectrum sunlight bounces harmlessly off the skin, while in another it penetrates right to the DNA of the cells, causing cancer. The frequencies that stimulate our retina pass through the atmosphere and are absorbed by the earth (as well as the retina); longer wavelengths pass through the earth and are absorbed by the atmosphere, which means that a retina sensitive to very long wavelengths could stare right through the planet to the bottom of the opaque atmosphere opposite, as if looking through an empty eggshell 8,000 miles in diameter. Another eye, sensitive to medium-length wavelengths, would see an opaque earth and a clear atmosphere, as we do, but there would be other wonders: images thrown from the far corners of the planet would dance about on the sky overhead, and shimmering moiré patterns of radio waves would hang between buildings like multicolored cobwebs. There would be two suns in the sky, the second being the galactic center (the center radiates on all frequencies, but interstellar dust absorbs those to which our retina is sensitive before they reach Earth.) A tourist wearing a pair of magic glasses, adjustable to any desired wavelength, would behold a new universe with every twist of the tuning knob.

From an engineering point of view, every specific electrical circuit has its own microniche in the spectrum, outside of which it stops working. By 1940 the relatively long wavelengths that were conducted by metal but insulated by air (that found air opaque but metal transparent) were well understood, being used to light bulbs and run motors and power electric heaters. The radio industry had been built on the medium wavelengths, to which air is transparent. Short wavelengths were still a terra incognita, partly because their properties were so exotic and delicate. Energy at these wavelengths behaves like sound; it is less conducted through wires than transmitted by and through geometries—tubes, horns, rectangular solids. Building a receiver or transmitter to handle these wavelengths requires a control over form as precise as that needed to design a good violin.

Until radar came along no point had been found at which the interests of humans and the properties of this exotic bestiary coincided. The tiny handful of physicists who had had an interest in these wavelengths before the war—mostly British to begin with—had been sucked up almost immediately by the Rad Lab's sister projects on the other side of the Atlantic. The Rad Lab therefore was forced into hiring on the basis of pretty minimal formal qualifications, like a little math and a willing attitude. Some who met those conditions were physicists and some were engineers; both groups reported to work, eager to leap far out into territory about which they knew almost nothing.

What happened then (certainly according to Institute folk history) was one of those historic events of delegitimization, like what the Great Depression did to Herbert Hoover. The stock strategy for navigating through solution space is to build a model and watch it fail. But generate-and-test only returns information if the experimental device produces some kind of performance, as inadequate as it might be. A plane can't crash without flying. Nothing can be learned from a device that just lies on the table with its legs in the air, version after version. And the behavior of microwave radiation was so fragile and delicate—like the performance of a professional violin—that over and over again the engineers couldn't get their designs to fly at all.

Of course neither could the physicists, in the beginning, but their professional inclination and temperament seemed better fitted to the situation. The stereotypical physicist's reflex response to a frustration was not to try to do something about it but to go off, sit down somewhere, and draw on mathematical tools to describe the problem as precisely and comprehensively as possible—to expand the context, widen the horizons. Again and again this approach suggested ideas, doors to try, while generate-and-test sat around mute as a piece of furniture. Without question there were Rad Lab engineers who picked up microwave instrument design as if born to it and physicists who spent the duration with their eyes crossed in confusion, but on balance the physicists kept cooking intellectually at much higher levels of ignorance than the engineers. When the collected achievements of the Rad Lab were published (in 26 volumes!) almost all the important papers were by physicists. "We were their [the physicists'] plumbers," one glum alum remembered ruefully. Presented with one of the great challenges in the history of engineering, the party of reality had had to be towed into action by the party of theory.

When the various engineering departments (and not just at MIT) took stock of the postwar world they concluded that the Rad Lab experience had been no fluke; the balance of performance between "reality" and "theory" had become permanently inverted. No doubt there were conservatives to point out that the incrementalist, industry-oriented system of engineering education had ratcheted American industry into the most productive in the world before the war and set near-miraculous records during the war itself, increasing production of warplanes and freighters by two orders of magnitude in three years. Was it sensible to declare a system bankrupt at the moment of its greatest success?

But from the perspective of the reform circles, that was then; the technologies emerging then were not just new tools but new disciplines, whole new branches of engineering that needed defining from the ground up. The new jet engine technology meant mechanical engineers would have to learn from scratch how to build machines that could operate at temperatures only three or four times cooler than the surface of the sun; most information on the new field of nuclear power engineering was classified, though even that was little enough. For engineers in these fields working under conditions of extreme novelty was inescapable; it was part of the job description.

Perhaps the most radical break with the historical engineering world view was associated with the invention of what appeared to be a perfectly general purpose machine, a device that (in theory) could execute any imaginable sequence of operation without any physical redesign, just by reading instructions, like a human. Of course somebody would have to write these instructions, and at least over the short term this person would have to be an engineer of a kind, but one who would be expert in the first purely abstract branch of engineering, the first to require no contact with physical parts.

The idea was naturally intriguing: physical parts wear and get dirty and are discontinued by their supplier and roll under the desk and are never made to the degree of precision promised by the catalog. They have to be attached to one another with glue or screws or solder and can take weeks to assemble and disassemble. Computers have their own headaches, but at least each and every bit and byte always performs exactly as advertised. When the programming goes well, sequences of instructions can be assembled and debugged in minutes or hours instead of weeks or months. Still, developing a branch of engineering divorced from real, physical shapes and materials was breaking new ground indeed.

Curiously enough, the computer had been conceived as a demonstration of the limits of mechanical procedure. In the early 1930s many professional mathematicians were wondering whether it could be shown that every mathematical assertion was solvable by a definite, mechanical, step-by-step procedure. The product of 28 and 34 can be calculated by a definite, mechanical procedure; the successive digits of pi can be worked out, one by one, by a definite, mechanical procedure. Can one extrapolate from these examples across the board, to the entire universe of mathematical objects? To many mathematicians the implications were disturbing. Since the entirety of mathematics can be seen as a single, very complicated proposition, if every mathematical supposition could be solved by some mechanical procedure, it would follow that somewhere out there was a procedure that could solve every problem, prove every theorem. If that were found, what would people need mathematicians for? "There is of course no such theorem," British mathematician G. H. Hardy once wrote, "and this is very fortunate, since if there were we should have a mechanical set of rules for the solution of all mathematical problems, and our activities as mathematicians would come to an end." Still, Hardy was basically whistling through the graveyard here, since when he wrote no one had proved the point.

One day in the spring of 1935 another British mathematician named Alan Turing jogged up the banks of the river Cam to a small town named Grantchester, cut into a field bordering on the highway, lay back, looked at the sky, and saw how to do so. The core of his idea was the implication of having calculations operate on themselves. Calculations usually come in two parts: procedures, and the objects that are moved around or combined by the procedures. Usually, again, these are written in two different languages: for instance, procedures might be written $+$, $-$, and $\times$, and objects 23, 41, and so on. But if procedures and objects were written in the same terminology, then a procedure could operate self-referentially. You could add the number for addition to itself.

The Austrian mathematician Kurt Gödel had shown in another context that the consequences of such logical mirroring were unpredictable—there was no way of proving what would happen when a sufficiently complex expression started eating its tail like this. Ergo, Turing concluded, there was at least one class of mathematical objects that could not be solved by a "mechanical set of rules": those in which the path out of the problem was the problem itself.

From the perspective of the professional mathematician the demonstration that mechanical procedures had their limits was a big result, but Turing saw that his work had even bigger and quite different implications outside mathematics. Writing both data and instructions in a common language meant that the computer could calculate and recalculate its own instructions as easily as an arithmetic problem. This made it infinitely flexible, and while, as Turing had shown, it might not be able to work through every procedure imaginable, the list of deterministic sequences that were not wrapped up in self-referential paradoxes was very long indeed. As Turing's biographer, Andrew Hodges, wrote, "Alan [not only] proved that there was no 'miraculous machine' that could solve all mathematical problems . . . he had discovered something almost [*sic!*] equally miraculous, the idea of a universal machine that could take over the work of *any* machine."

On the most general level, a useful computer consists of a device that translates physical changes into symbols, a processor that runs a list of instructions on the symbols, and an "actuator" that returns the symbols emerging from the processor back into physical changes.

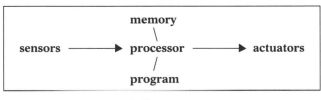

A Computer

In real life the sensor and actuator represented in the graphic are usually humans: one group of people transforms a real-world condition into data, perhaps by banging on a keyboard, while some other group translates the processor output back into changes in the real world, for instance by sending out bills. (Of course the sensors and actuators can also be machines themselves.)

So for instance, imagine a ball rolling over the floor from point A to B to C (the ball might be a machine used to knock down bowling pins). The sensors are at A, the actuators at B, and the judges observing this whole operation are at C. If the sensors correctly measure the speed and direction of the ball as it leaves A, and if the right physics has been written into the program, then the processor should be able to calculate what the speed and direction of the ball will be as it rolls past B. In fact, if the original ball were thrown away at A (after the measurements had been made) and a different ball fired off at B at a speed and in a direction consistent with these calculations, no one looking at the ball as it went past C would be able to tell the difference. The computer would have replaced or taken over or modeled the ball's motion, with all its friction and vibration and texture, between A and B. You could move those points further apart, perhaps taking over the throwing of the ball in the first place, or of its knocking over the bowling pins on the other end. In theory, the observers at C should not be able to tell if you had or not.

In theory, the sensors and actuators could be moved far enough apart to encompass the whole world of engineering. To do that would require that computers be capable of doing whatever humans could do, and at least as well, but most of the early workers in this field couldn't see why that should be a problem. "It is not my aim to surprise or shock," systems theorist Herbert Simon wrote in 1957, "[but] there are now in the world machines that think, that learn, and that create. Moreover, their ability to do these things is going to increase rapidly until—in a visible future—the range of problems they can handle will be coextensive with that to which the human mind has been applied."

Turing himself saw no obstacle to building a machine at least intelligent enough to hold up its end in conversation with a group of British academics (which to an American seems a pointlessly high standard). To be exact, he saw no obstacle other than the sheer tedium of programming in the text of the *Encyclopædia Brittanica*; once provided with that tool to the interpretation of the cosmos, all the lofty philosophical commentary and wealth of literary reference should flow out by itself. Perhaps even simpler approaches might be possible, Turing speculated, such as writing out the program for a child's brain and sending it to school:

> *Presumably the child-brain is something like a notebook as one buys it from the stationers. Rather little mechanism, and lots of blank sheets. . . . Our hope is that there is so little mechanism in the child-brain that something like it can be easily programmed.*

Not that this method would be entirely simple:

> *It will not be possible to apply exactly the same teaching process to the machine as to a normal child . . . one could not send the creature to school without the other children making excessive fun of it. It must be given some tuition . . ."*

Whatever the implications of computers for human employment, clearly the machine portended profound changes for engineering. In 1950 MIT scrapped the Dynamo Lab (and its equivalents in the other departments) and commenced to reimagine itself as a center of something called the "engineering sciences."

The engineering and natural sciences have the same tools but differ in their ends. The natural sciences will have worked themselves out of business when they can answer any question about the underlying logic of the natural order; the end of the engineering sciences is a collection of principles from which the design of every artifact both physically possible and desirable by our species can be calculated without appeal to generate-and-test: a unified theory of solution space.

The final product of the natural sciences is an oracle; of the engineering sciences, Aladdin's lamp. The engineering sciences can also be seen as another branch of engineering, another sort of tool building, in which the products are logical machines—formulas, models—instead of items of hardware like a bridge or a car, and where the clients are the engineering professions themselves instead of industry.

As an example of the beast, suppose we needed to design something that could hold water on a stove top while bringing it to a boil. One path to a solution might be to make a model, see how it worked, bang out a second, and so on; a second would be to calculate the materials and geometries appropriate for any given boiling situation, so that the design emerged from the calculations instead of actual experience. Engineering science is the business of developing such formulae. In this example an engineering scientist would begin by teasing apart all the factors influencing boiling behavior (i.e., the amount of water in the pot, the caloric output of the heating element, time on the burner, the efficiency of heat transfer from the heating element to the bottom of the pot, the heat conductivity of the materials, room temperature, the thermal behavior of the solutes present in the water, the rate at which the pot loses heat through convection and/or infrared radiation, ambient air pressure, and so on) and the constants controlling the interaction of those factors. Next the weakest points in the current edifice of boiling theory— the points where the design uncertainties were greatest— would be isolated and a research program devised that would promise some prospect of reducing them. Grant applications would be mailed; any monies returning (after the Institute's deduction for overhead costs; currently around 60 percent of the gross) would go to hiring graduate students to build the instruments to generate the data that would support integrating the next order of complexity into the logic of boiling water.

With luck the engineering scientist would eventually develop a formula, a logical mobile, in which all the factors hung in their proper relationship. This formula might or might not be "practical": finding the right input values to the proper levels of precision might require thousands of dollars of instrument time, the math might be far more demanding than the norm for the field, and the formula would probably have nothing to say about the ergonomics of using pots or cost-effective pot manufacture or how long a given pot might last with normal treatment—all being issues of "development" and therefore better left in the lap of industry. But *International Boiling Systems Research Abstracts B* would gobble it up.

The engineering sciences were no twentieth-century invention: Galileo made one of the first contributions to the genre when he derived and published formulas for scaling the building models of architects to full-size. Another early but representative venture was the systematic exploration by French engineers in the early nineteenth century of the properties of all the possible proportions in the ingredients of concrete. The MIT Chemical Engineering Department was reorganized around the engineering sciences in the 1920s, dropping a focus on the machinery used to handle specific chemicals for a transindustrial perspective on general processes like heating, evaporating, mixing, transporting, and the like. Still, such examples were not common, since the experiments necessary to generate the data and validate whatever generalizations suggested themselves were seldom cheap. Most of the prewar experience in the engineering sciences had been realized in industries in which the generate-and-test design mode was prohibitively expensive. (As in building oil refineries.) Before World War II it would have been impossible for a low-rent operation running on tuition and donated equipment, as MIT had been, to support the equipment and manpower costs of a modern engineering theory shop even had it wanted to.

After the war, anything seemed possible. The nation and its government were as convinced as anyone at the Institute that enormous changes were imminent. The general opinion expressed in popular magazines like *Collier's* and *Look* was that "scientists" were men of such puissance that they could come up with innovations like jet engines, radar, nuclear power, computers, or DDT at any time, on request. All these had prewar roots, but at that time innovations were thought to come either from industry or independent inventors, like Edison. The war had shown where the golden eggs were being laid, and the government was determined to use its funding powers to follow up on this discovery. After all, the Communists were out there feeling around as well.

The military research bureaucracies tried to channel this funding into their own facilities, but were crushed by Vannevar Bush, Roosevelt's science advisor, an ex-MIT provost and a master of the bureaucratic game. Whatever other politics might have been involved, on a public policy level an academic research environment has the advantage over a private research contractor or government laboratory of training new manpower, thereby contributing to the security of the nation independently of the results of any specific project. (Academies also can generate more paper, and more prestigious-looking paper, than nonacademic researchers.) During the 1940s the number of government-sponsored projects at MIT rose from the dozens into the hundreds.

There was nothing incremental about these projects. The U.S. government was looking for major strides, breakthroughs like self-repairing machinery; power from sea water; ultra-high-speed manufacturing processes; rockets;

machine vision; high-performance materials that were superhard, vibration resistant, heat resistant, and corrosion-free; tanks that could read a map; and navigation systems that could take a missile around the world and drop it on a given street address. To those standing on the threshold of the nuclear age it seemed reckless to declare any question beyond the reach of a 10- or even 5-year development effort. Besides, only great leaps in technology would compensate for the tsunami of Communist troops that were expected to roll across Europe or over the Bering Straits at any moment. Finally, the alternative, funding projects of immediate industrial relevance with public money, raised difficult questions about fueling profits with taxes from the left, or intervening in the market by funding research that would end by favoring one group of competitors over another from the right. The decision to concentrate on the most ambitious, long-range questions followed naturally.

The transition to the engineering sciences moved the center of cultural gravity of the Institute from issues of design and function to questions about the "natural behavior of artifacts," about the relation of the geometry of surfaces to the propagation of cracks, the effects of temperature stress on electrical components, the behavior of construction materials during earthquakes, the association of the properties of threads to those of the fabrics woven from those threads, the distribution of heat during welding, the variation in rope strength in salt water over varying regimes of abrasion, the influence of gravity on casting processes, the modeling of vibration, noise, and wear in high-performance machine systems, and so on. Such questions differ from questions of design in that the number of ways a given set of design specifications can be satisfied is very large (in theory, infinite), while there is never more than one right answer to a properly defined question about nature. Making a "contribution" in science is not like making a painting that would never have existed without your efforts; the only uncertainty about scientific answers is when they will be found and by whom. You make a contribution in science precisely by making it before Schmidt in Chicago or Vianelli in Turin or Matsui in Tsukuba, since journals do not publish solutions to problems to which everybody has known the answer for months.*

Of course in any design project moments come when only one answer seems possible (at best!), and scientific results often require many revisions and confirmations. But there remains a difference, and one expression of this difference is that the Institute became dramatically more expensive to run. Though theorists—intellects who appear to need nothing but paper and a blackboard—are the celebrities of science, in fact the lab with the best tools will win almost every race almost every time. (Especially since the best tools attract the best people.) Any lab getting into science, and therefore declaring itself a competitor in at least some of these races, has to be prepared for large-scale, continuing investments in buying, building, and maintaining instruments that reach right to the edge of the measurable and in the labor needed to maintain and operate them. The operating expenses of MIT increased 700 percent between 1940 (when it was $3 million) and 1950; they have been climbing ever since. (Research expenses alone came close to $300 million in 1991.) This is the bill the government (largely) picks up, paradoxically paying the same category of costs at

---

*The competitive pressures were also intensified by a shift in who could declare a specific question important or interesting. Before the war, this right belonged to a heterogeneous group of companies, each with its distinctive set of market relations; postwar, to academic bodies with a consensus on how to rank the significance of the outstanding problems. The effect was to make the bull's-eye much clearer.

Stanford, Carnegie-Mellon, Los Alamos, and several other laboratories and institutes that got into engineering sciences at the same time and were all competing with each other.

Scientists occasionally deny that science is competitive, by which they mean only that the approved direction for competitive stress is inward, that it is to be applied in twisting the mind and character to whatever pitch is required to stay in the pack or, as in the case of MIT, near the front. There is a term in ecology for the (speculative) situation in which a complex of interacting species, an entire ecology, is thrown into an evolutionary phase such that its members simultaneously undergo rapid, open-ended, adaptive change. In these conditions a species filling any given ecological role (parasite, predator, scavenger) must change continually, generation after generation, just to stay in the same ecological niche. This is called the "Red Queen strategy." Whether it exists in nature or not, it is surely the dominant rhythm of the supercharged, flat-out, atmosphere of the corridors.

Though engineering science is not an undergraduate game, the consequences of these changes percolated even to that end of the curriculum. The pleasures of working on real machines were exchanged for those of grinding out problem sets based on the equations for thermodynamics, electrodynamics, statistical mechanics, parameter estimations, sampling distributions, confidence intervals, and other issues of comparable abstraction in the modeling and analysis of "engineering systems." An alumni who attended MIT in the 1960s remembers that the transition drew a clear line between the students oriented to working with real machines that led out into society—who were left blinking with confusion—and the mathematically oriented types for whom one set of units, one set of problems, was just like another. These sailed on ahead. The archive photos testify that when the big machines left campus, they took the suits with them: the students in the lab photos of the 1950s wear wrinkled chinos and white shirts open at the collar. They seem slightly goofier, more kinetic, and much younger. They smile more and let their jaws hang open, sometimes slightly, sometimes more than slightly. They look like nerds.

On the one hand this is as might be expected, since the term arose in the 1960s to refer, in part, to students still dressing in the fashion of the previous decade. On the other, the nerd is such a major figure in the mythology of MIT that finding a photo of an authentic sample is like stumbling over a record of a unicorn or leprechaun. Certainly central casting would be hard pressed to cast the role from the traffic in the Infinite Corridor in this decade; the fashions here are global student fashionlessness: black T-shirts, tennis shoes, turtlenecks, black or blue denims, sweats over leggings, corduroys, canvas backpacks. High fashion is represented by the occasional pair of baggy hiphop pants. Any short-sleeved pointy-collared Orlon shirt passing through the corridors these days would almost certainly be intended ironically, as a fashion quote, perhaps as part of a student comedy or campaign stunt.

One element of the nerd concept (as it is used by the world at large) denotes an inability to tune into affect, to divine states of feeling or respect the authority of the subjective sensibility. The archetypal nerd has neither the capacity to detect nor any willingness to act on changes in the emotional atmosphere, partly because such weather is beneath the notice of a rational intelligence. He (the stereotypical nerd is male) is therefore always inappropriately engaged, asking nuns if they wear bras, speculating about embalming technology during funerals, hammering away on subjects everyone tired of hours ago, pronouncing ideas of general interest "meaningless," and pouncing viciously on any utterance he thinks of as an error of fact, no matter how trivial and irrelevant to the discussion.

It is true that a person walking into MIT might well feel the culture bending a degree or two in this direction. As compared to the general population, eye contact might be a bit more glancing and the role of facial expression, voice tone, and body language narrowed a touch. The style lends itself to precision, interruption, and contradiction. It does have an edge. Once a graduate student offered to explain why MIT types tended to hang together at parties. If you just wander around at random, he said, "People come up and ask questions like 'How do you like Boston?'" He cited the query in a tone of indignant ridicule. "What does *that* mean? How am I supposed to answer a question like *that*?"

There is nothing new in this style, however; at least for most of this century nobody ever wasted the best china on engineers. Until the 1950s the cultural image of engineers was of direct, plain-spoken, chivalric, quiet men who wore field boots and wide leather belts, kept their flannel shirts open to the clavicle, and went through a lot of beer. (The cultural historian Bruce Sinclair reports that virtually every film made in the 1920s about engineers featured Gary Cooper types.) At some point after the war this archetype was replaced by the image, witheringly drawn to a remarkable level of detail, of a scrawny (or dumpy) fellow with the physical stamina of an old man, noisy habits of respiration, and a crew cut topping a white-flour complexion peppered with acne rosettes.

Everybody, somehow, figured out that a nerd wears khaki cotton pants that are both high enough in the leg to flash the white socks he wears with his heavy black shoes and large enough in the waist so that the material wads up under his shiny black plastic belt; that he carries a fully loaded white plastic pen-pak in the pocket of a white short-sleeved pointy-collared Orlon shirt open to a white T-shirt lying over a rice-paper skin; and that his glasses have Coke-bottle lenses and black plastic frames that carry a history of repair—Scotch tape, paper clips, safety pins—like medals on a dictator's chest.*

Fashion is a text and it is not hard to read the message in the nerd look: these engineers are sexless, eunuchs, terminally prepubescent (the look also prescribes seven inches of loose belt hanging down over the fly as a facetious, teasing, counterpoint to this very sexlessness). This story was articulated in quasi-academic fashion by an MIT psychosociologist named Sherry Turkle in a book called *The Second Self*. Turkle argued that the very act of building tools (she is especially suspicious of contact with computers) disrupts the relationship of mind and body, alienating the engineer from his physical self and triggering a general crisis of self-esteem. Turkle cites the testimony of a junior, "Ron," who confesses to a lengthy personal history of concern over his physical attractiveness. "Ron's sense of himself as ugly is not supported in any way by his physical inheritance, although it is well supported by his grooming and gait," Turkle observes unsparingly, summarizing: "He sees the power of his mind as a gift that brought him mastery over technology, but for which he has to pay with shame and misery in the world of people." Ron represents what she claims is a "widespread presence of what has to be described as self-loathing" in the MIT student body, though it is not clear why a reader should be impressed by the discovery of a college junior who wished he looked better. Turkle's argument also includes a few paragraphs devoted to an annual reverse beauty contest

---

*One excellent representation of the stereotype was laid out by Alexander Theroux in the October 1986 issue of *New England Monthly*.

held yearly to pick "the ugliest man on campus." "They flaunt their pimples, their pasty complexions, their knobby knees, their thin undeveloped bodies . . ." she writes in a tone that crosses more than halfway to disgust, clearly seeing the rite as some kind of denial through overcompensation.

The n-term is not uncommon at MIT, but here it has a different meaning, referring to those who let the circulation of connections carry them off without worrying about the depth of the water or rumors of sharks, who make no compromises for comfort or career. There are craft nerds, who insist on tying up every loose end exactly so, and concept nerds, who sail off after radically interesting but totally untested design ideas, and even execution nerds, who reach for design solutions that instead of just relaxing a given constraint, kill it dead, erase it so utterly from the list of concerns that no one coming after them will ever think of it. In all these cases the righteous nerd puts more of himself into the effort than is sensible or prudent. He gives too much; he can't hold back. (The programmers at the Chinese restaurant who felt they had to rewrite the cash register code were this sort of nerd.) At MIT the nerd term permits, encourages, and rationalizes these acts of self-indulgence. Whenever a student is faced with the temptation to do more than he really should, to leave his own private mark, his taste, his sense of art, on solution space, the devil will whisper in his ear: "You can't expect to live your life like an accountant. You're a nerd! Do it!" And he will. The idea behind the "Ugliest Man" contest is to celebrate, through parody, release from the lookist, cosmetic tensions of high school. You're at MIT, the contest is supposed to be saying, a nerd among nerds. At least while you're here nobody is going to be mocking your haircut. Your shame and misery payments are in abeyance—until graduation.

I know of no explanation for this shift in the opinion of the culture on the sexual resources of engineers. One speculation is that it reflects a growing anxiety in the 1960s over the sociosexual consequences of rapid technological change. Suppose computers really did take over, as so many seemed to think? Presumably the largest share of social power would then flow to their interlocutors, the engineers, who might use it as men have always used social power, to assure unlimited access to the sexual resources of the society. The nerd myth compensates for these fears through a kind of preemptive castration by wish-fulfillment, gelding these potential competitors through stereotype as unworthy of and even uninterested in social and sexual power, and incompetent to compete for them in any case.

There are other possibilities, of course. Farms have been high-technology, tool-centered environments for thousands of years, contexts in which the legitimacy of the design and construction of tools was beyond question. When the center of the culture moved to suburbia, away from both farms and industrial centers, to communities where tools are either brought by a contractor or bought at Sears, an interest in that activity might have seemed more problematic, incomplete, and dispensable. There is some dim echo of that in the pictures of MIT undergraduates of the 1950s, seated as they are in the looming absence of the great machines of the past, like the memory of a demolished building hanging over a parking lot.

Redefining itself around the engineering sciences did not make MIT into a pencil-and-paper shop; the machine shops were as busy as ever, though now with the construction and rebuilding of instruments. In all other respects the transformation ran from crown to root. MIT went from a low-cost undergraduate school whose major client was industry, major product the journeyman engineer, and major emphasis the incremental improvements of real machines to (primarily) a graduate institution, dependent on government money to defray much higher expenses, whose product was contributions to the engineering logic of highly speculative, even visionary projects.

The engineering schools of most of the other countries around the world have stuck with incremental, industry-oriented tweaking, and the record of their performance (as in Japan, Korea, Taiwan, and Hong Kong) suggests that when MIT made its jump it left a lot of meat on the old bones. It is not clear that the innovative record of the last third of this century is the equal of either the first (airplanes, radio, movies, the industrial production of cars, the bulldozer) or the second (antibiotics, television, jet aircraft, the transistor, computers, integrated circuits, photocopying, the laser), let alone their superior.* Of the success stories of the terminal third of our century—the VCR, the compact disk, the FAX, the spreadsheet, the telephone answering machine—only the microprocessor seems clearly in the same league. The engineering sciences have accumulated a remarkable body of knowledge, but the rate of introduction of significant new tools seems to be slowing.

If the productivity of engineering, as measured by the number of big new ideas, is in fact slowing, the direct cause is hardly likely to be the direction along which a few elite institutions have chosen to channel their energies. (A more likely category of explanation would be the shift away from a tool-centered, agricultural culture to a society whose young

---

*Comparing just the technologies with which the average member of the population is likely to have had contact.

engineers get their ideas about physical reality from television.) Still, the productivity of engineering is certainly the Institute's business, and it might not be synchronized properly with its time. But this is only its second build-and-test cycle; MIT has its own regions of solution space to explore, and by any standard that process can only have just begun.

The Tech
Model Railroad Club

When the war ended the government handed the Rad
Lab over to the Institute to do with as it wished. This
huge infusion of new resources so deflated the political cost
of floor space (for a few months) that a few square feet was
doled out to poor relatives in linguistics and psychology. (Perhaps not entirely coincidentally, among these were a number
of professors—Noam Chomsky, Jerome Weisner, Jerry Lettvin, and others—whose broad interests, speculative gifts, wit,
presence, and command of the culture lifted Building 20 to a
modest reputation as MIT's Left Bank.) A thousand square feet
of this distribution to the margin went to MIT's Model Railroad Club, which until then had had to beg space off campus.

Though the Club was obviously not MIT's first priority,
the considerations that inclined Facilities Management to

grant its petition are easy to guess. With all its bridges, buildings, roads, factories, and mines, model railroading is an extended memorialization of engineering, specifically including the tremendous intelligence that went into railroad technology itself. Nor was it impossible that the Club would hit on some useful new extensions of the art, forming the same relation to the model railroad industry, to Lionel and American Flyer, that MIT had had (but was abandoning) with other industrial sectors.

But so far as its members were concerned, the Tech Model Railroad Club (TMRC, pronounced Tee-Merck) was more an alternative to MIT than an extension of it. The whole point of the hobby is to escape some unpleasant reality, to fly from the "real world" into a flow of train-related fantasies. When a fan puts his head down on the layout and a train comes clattering up into his face, that train boosts him into another life. It might be his own past: he could be groping for the moment when he first saw a locomotive flowing over the horizon, rising up like a mountain, reaching forward like an opening fist. He might be looking to reexperience just a taste of that delicious indecision between staring right into the face of the onrushing spectacle and hiding in his parent's side, of the first sensation of personal bravery, even a triumphant identification between the momentum of that hurtling force and the rising arc of his own youth.

This is perhaps the primal model railroad fantasy, but there are others, like traveling out to all the corners of the continent, or hammering 35,000 horses through the countryside, graciously accepting the deference of the cars drawn up at intersections with the self-confidence that comes with riding one of the big pistons of the industrial engine, or living in a certain landscape or time or society, like a mountain village, a tough, adult, industrial cityscape, or Eisenhower's Indiana. In theory these same visions might be drawn or painted on paper or canvas, but building them in three dimensions and snaking a moving train through the dioramas vivifies them, conveying a sense of a society beyond the borders of the piece, a degree of autonomous purpose, of independence, that provokes and attracts the imagination. Still another fantasy is participating in the net of industrial connectivity, of devising and managing the intricate pattern of exchanges of gases, oils, syrups, slurries, pigments, acids, solvents, sands, pulpwood, I-beams, rolls of tin stock, everything down to and including junk and ashes and dust, all the offstage activities that comprise the recipe for industrial civilization. Ninety-nine citizens out of a hundred, if that few, are completely oblivious to all these interactions, but for a handful this ramifying matrix is one of the great vistas of our day. And finally, perhaps most relevant in this case, there is the engineering fantasy: that of building bridges, rail lines, stations, roads, warehouses, and tunnels; of moving across the widest stretches of professional possibility.

Nothing could be more natural than that the members of a breakneck culture like the Institute's, where any wave can wipe you out, should need a back door like this. TMRC was a combination fraternal organization, neighborhood bar, wilderness hut, and safe house, an oasis of communitas in a culture that otherwise held its members up to the most scary sort of individual inspection. The members of TMRC understood this, semiconsciously, treating one another as tenderly as was possible in a time and place in which only psychiatrists spoke freely about "emotional needs." They addressed the problems of social reward and discipline by bestowing "smiles" and "frowns" on fellow members. ("Motion that a frown be levied on X for his persistent disregard of proper equipment maintenance.")

People were forever slipping into the Club after midnight to wire up the relays to amuse the members with some weird effect, like a train running into a tunnel and seeming to vanish, or triggering strange noises on the track or around the clubroom. (These were called "hacks," a term that was to have a distinguished future.) "The idea was to spread 'wonder and awe,'" a member said years later, projecting the tone of an official slogan into the last three words. A significant fraction of those wandering in and out of the clubroom were not members—even had no interest in trains—but random students looking to unwind in its happy and sheltered pandemonium with a quick fix of bridge or hearts.

Perhaps the most important service the Club offered its members was the gift of a sphere of action in which the stakes were low; in which it was possible to just *be*. Many students arrive at MIT having defined themselves around their competence on technical issues since they were 10 and expecting—hoping—to do so for the rest of their lives. What they look for from the university is not only an education but an affirmation of their life's core, an opinion on whether they really are who they think they are, an advisory that MIT is uniquely qualified to give (they think). In this context, any grade less than an A makes your past look that much more pretentious and your future that much less promising. And even if you do get an A on one problem set, the next one sets your life in play again.

TMRC allowed its members to put that last disastrous thermo problem set behind them and actually build something of immediate use to themselves and their friends. It was a world where a person could take a breath free from the incessant judging and measuring that plagued the soul in the "real world" of the lab and classroom. Besides, there was no denying that an undergraduate was likely to do more actual physical designing and building in the Club than anywhere else in the Institute, preoccupied as it was with "models of engineering" and "engineering systems."

From certain perspectives it was not totally clear which side of the border was more involved in make-believe. Designing a layout required weaving all the fantasies listed above into the history and nature of trains, their natural and social environments, the crafts of miniaturization and visual illusion, the mechanics of small objects and low-frequency electrical circuits, low-level (sometimes high-level) signaling and switching logic, practical considerations like ease of maintenance, accessibility, and cost, together with the schedules, skills, and interests of a heterogeneous group. If engineering was the integration of logically incompatible levels of reality into tools, model railroading qualified abundantly, on every level.

Collectively the members of TMRC had still another fantasy of trains: the metafantasy of making the fantasies themselves start sooner, gather in more issues, cut deeper, last longer; to advance the state of the brain-train connection, ideally running it off into some territory altogether new. In effect they were fantasy engineers, working to supercharge these dreams of trains. A bodacious TMRC modeler slapping his face down on the track might be projecting himself into the layout like any fan, or he might be twisting his imagination around on itself, trying to recreate the state of mind of a person projecting himself into the scene, picking up the resonances of having been "snatched," of standing there with a slack jaw and glassy eyes, out-of-body, vanished; of experiencing wonder and awe. Perhaps therefore the most useful analogy of all for the Tech Model Railroad Club is that of a prisoner-of-war camp in which the inmates are organizing a mass escape—some through tunnels, some through the fences, some hidden in trucks, whatever, the important point being that everyone is working on getting everyone else out. When the power went on and the trains began to move, the whole Club went out-of-campus *ensemble*, or at least that was the intention.

Most of the Club's energies were wrapped up in moving to higher and higher degrees of realism. A new member might learn how the distribution of temperature in a steam engine or a given period of service affects the patterns of weathering on the engine box, or how to lay a little flare of rust down the engine casing to mark the "sweat" exuded by the steam whistle and bell. He might be taught that highway asphalt is not black but grey, or the proper sequence of shades expressed by the gravel at various distances from a railyard, or how the region of the country a freight car has arrived from, has rolled through, affects the color of the dust coating its sides (dust is important because real railroads never clean their freight cars). He might learn how to build up grading and lay track with tiny spikes the size of whiskers.

In the 1950s the members of the Club started to focus on a single problem: controlling two or more trains on the same track independently. Model railroads (usually) control acceleration by varying the electric power through the track as a whole. Push the throttle and every train on the layout will speed up; pull it back and all will slow. This lockstep synchrony throws a barrier across a whole range of escapist train fantasies. A real train complex—in the locution of the model trade, a "prototype"—is made up of several different kinds of train behaviors and interactions: there are passenger trains, express freights, through freights (which travel from city to city), and way freights (which distribute cars locally, from siding to siding). Each has its own routines and responsibilities, its own distinctive category of engineer, and therefore its own peculiar hallucinations of authenticity.

Further, the inability to support different operating schedules simultaneously foreclosed the most interesting flight of fancy, that of dispatcher. This commanding presence is the general of connectivity, the commander of trains, the authority who defines the timetable and adds or subtracts trains or schedules "meets," those occasions when cars are swapped from one locomotive to another. Given the analogy between locomotive engineers and musicians, a connection some are willing to make, the role of dispatcher transforms naturally into orchestral conductor. Finally, and perhaps conclusively, central control is incompatible with good fellowship.

The traditional fix attempted by other clubs (and by TMRC until the mid-1950s) was to wire up a large bank of toggle switches at each control station such that power controlled from that station could be switched to any section of track. If the layout were divided (for example) into four sections, then each console would have eight on/off toggle switches, each labeled with a different section number and direction of travel. Imagine, for instance, that train X is running through section 1. We would flip the switches into the following pattern:

	Section 1	**Section 2**	**Section 3**	**Section 4**
clockwise:	on ◀ off	on ▶ off	on ▶ off	on ▶ off
countercw:	on ▶ off	on ▶ off	on ▶ off	on ▶ off

This series of settings would switch the wires underneath the layout so that the flow of power looked like this (O is a second train being controlled from B to illustrate the principle of multiple centers of control):

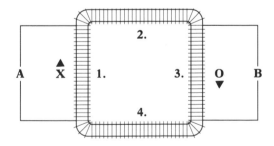

Separate banks of switches are needed for clockwise and counterclockwise travel because (high performance) model trains move in the direction of the flow of current. If we wanted X to run over 1 counterclockwise, for instance, to make it back up, we would flip the toggles this way:

	Section 1	Section 2	Section 3	Section 4
clockwise:	on ▶ off	on ▶ off	on ▶ off	on ▶ off
countercw:	on ◀ off	on ▶ off	on ▶ off	on ▶ off

which in actual connections means:

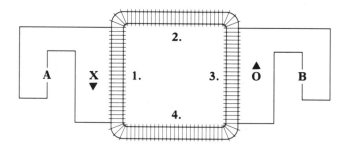

When X and O arrive in sections 2 and 4, traveling clockwise, we will flip the toggles to reconnect the wires under the layout to look like this:

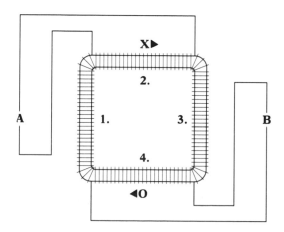

When X runs into 3 . . .

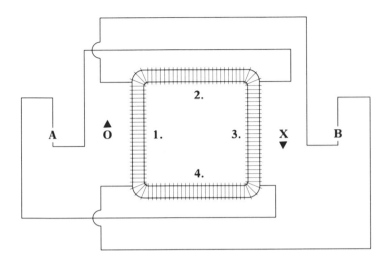

And so on.

In theory a layout wired like this could control up to four trains at the same time, each from a different station, but in practice all that switching and monitoring crushed the juice out of the most robust fantasy life. By 1950 model railroad clubs had been speculating for years about a system that would carry the right commands to the right train automatically, no matter where on the layout it might be, but so far without progress. "It was the sort of thing the average model railroader just dreamed about," a member from those years said.

Such a system would have been built up out of a device called a relay, which is a circuit that controls the behavior of some other circuit, perhaps by sending power to an electro-mechanical switch that physically opens or closes the wires composing the "slave" circuit. Relays are a flexible piece of machinery—you can have relays controlling relays controlling relays—and by midcentury ways had been found to make these machines produce remarkably complicated

behavior. The most technically dramatic example was the
phone system itself, but more accessible instances appeared
from time to time. In the early 1950s an MIT alumnus and
future faculty member named Claude Shannon even built a
maze solver out of relays—a mechanical lab rat. (Shannon's
intention was to comment on the controversy of whether
machines could be said to learn.) Relays stimulated ideas
like these; they were thought-like in a way unusual among
tools, naturally bending the mind toward ambitions like
modeling the flow of cognitive processes. Consider the following examples:

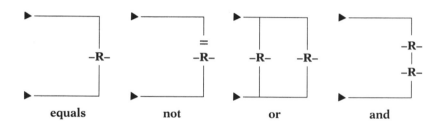

In all these cases a relay (R) affects the behavior of some
other circuit (not shown). In the first case, turning on the
relay completes the second circuit, allowing current to flow;
in the second, turning on the relay breaks the second circuit;
in the third, either of two relays can complete the other
circuit; in the fourth, both relays need to be on to accomplish
the same end. These four circuits, respectively, are homolo-
gous to the conjunctions "equals," "not," "or," and "and"
that we use in deliberative, instrumental, thought. A person
framing the thought, "if A and B or C are true, but either D or
E are not, then F should happen" can map this thought
directly into relay architecture, using logical modules like
those immediately above to ensure that when all the preliminary conditions are met, circuit F will come alive. The

analogy is not perfect—there is more to thinking than stringing together sequences of conjunctions—but conjunctions are conspicuous elements in logical thinking; they express the branching points, the nodes of transformation, of the semantic flow. Of course every tool expresses the thinking absorbed by its design, but relay circuits did so more explicitly and intimately, which is why the industry called them "logic elements." These would be the basic modules in any progressive cab control design; the logical equivalents of a roofing nail or 2x4 board.

Development of an automatic multiple control system was blocked from two sides, the first being complexity: an automatic switching system would have to sense the location and direction of motion of all the trains running on the layout, combine that information with signals coming from the control panels and other track sections and signals in the layout, and then switch into the right wiring configuration out of thousands of possibilities instantly and accurately. Designing the circuit this capable and flexible was like solving a London *Times* puzzle a hundred yards on a side: it could be done, but it was slow and exacting work.

The second problem was reliability; whatever the circuit design happened to be, it would certainly require thousands of relays, and that meant that unless the error and breakdown rate per relay was vanishingly small, the modelers would be spending 100 percent of their time fixing the system and 0 percent actually running trains. If the average relay failed after a year of continual operation, and there were 3650 relays in the design, which was not an unrealistic number, then on average 10 relays would break every day. This was obviously intolerable; there was no point in even starting to think about circuit design unless the basic module could work continually for a decade, and preferably two, without failing.

The phone company made relays with these levels of durability, but they were right at state of the art, and their costs, especially in the required quantities, would have represented a capital expenditure far in excess of anything any club could afford. Then in the mid-1950s the executive officer of the Electrical Engineering Department, Carleton Tucker, opened his mail to discover a letter from Western Electric announcing its intention to begin distributing surplus stocks to the leading electrical engineering departments around the country *without charge*. By fortunate coincidence Tucker was also the faculty advisor of the TMRC. He routed the catalog directly to the members, who tore through it like spies going through a purloined codebook.

Pages of relays were being offered. The club put in for them all, and to their delight, got them all—apparently no other institution was interested in that component. The same thing happened the next year, and the year after that. For the life of the program, TMRC received the entire excess of Western Electric's relay inventory. Many are stored to this day, piled in boxes stacked under the layout, gorgeous instruments in ceramic and brass, ranging in size from dominoes and bricks to small bookcases, glimmering with the condensed intelligence of man-centuries of effort by AT&T's relay engineers.

The quality of these relays allowed TMRC to begin building the first progressive cab control system in the history of model railroading. As the years rolled on (the project took 10 years), the members began to develop a sense of a logical landscape rising in and around and over the physical landscape of the actual layout. While relays can be compared to the flow of logical thoughts, every human mind has a ceiling to the complexity of the logical structure it is able to control. Relays can be built to any level of complexity. They allowed a person to set ideas down and build them up, week after week, into dense, involute, complexly textured, stable logic machines no engineer alive could have held in mind.

Relays made little snaps or clicks when they worked, so a designer with an educated ear could sit next to a relay circuit and listen to the relays stepping through the same chain of logic used to analyze the problem. Sometimes you forgot whether the clicks were marking events that were inside or outside the brain, and at those moments, as the sounds of the relays lit up the logical structure, you could feel the whole circuit design all at once, as a single enormous idea, reaching out in all directions, both inside and outside your mind, and bigger than any other idea you had had in your life.

In these terms the phone company was the biggest idea in the history of civilization, and Club members began making inspection tours of New England Telephone relay stations just as they did train stations and depots and yards. Today the switching load required to handle the calls of a region like New England can be managed with a machine the size of a refrigerator, but in those days relay stations were set in rooms the size of high school gymnasiums. A dozen or two relay banks, each hundreds of square feet in area and six inches thick and holding tens of thousands of relays, hung from the ceiling like quilts from the beds of giants hung out to dry. The members of TMRC, whose reputation opened many doors, would walk into these spaces, thread their way through the thin walls of relays, talk to the engineers, and soak in the storms of clicks and snaps gusting from Cambridge and Somerville, New York City and Washington D.C. They got so good at listening to these forest noises that occasionally they even picked up on anomalies before the AT&T engineers did, like Indians catching the sound of a train laboring from 30 miles away.

As flexible as relays were, the TMRC members were acutely aware that they were not the optimal logic element.

Relays could be configured and reconfigured a lot faster than purely mechanical elements, but reorganizing the constellation of relations, experimenting with a new "cognitive structure," still required a lot of hand wiring. There was an alternative technology out there, one representing as big an increase in flexibility and power over relays as Western Electric's relays had been over the devices sold in hobby stores: the digital computer. The computer was like a relay bank where all you had to do was type the pattern of connections into the machine and it would wire itself to your design automatically. It was as different from the relay as casting or carving printing plates was from composing them from movable type.

Unfortunately, during the 1950s run time on the few computers on the MIT campus was so expensive that only the best-endowed research projects could buy more than an hour or two, and the biggest sponsor, the military, demanded stringent access control as a condition of doing business at all. Even in that climate it might have been possible to arrange time for students—MIT was supposed to be an educational institution—but the academic authorities saw no reason to make room in the curriculum. Nobody denied that circumstances might arise in which it would be useful to know programming, but the same could be said of shorthand or carpentry or reading upside down. The right question was, was programming an engineering science? Did it have a theoretical underpinning? Did the field have "fundamentals," or anyway enough to justify a course? A considerable body of opinion thought not (it has its adherents to this day), which meant that even as late as 1958 MIT did not offer a single programming course.

In 1959 the Department of Electrical Engineering finagled a long-term loan of a computer from Lincoln Labs, an MIT-affiliated facility organized around defense work. The

TX-O had its strong points—it was one of the first computers to display results on a screen instead of using punch cards—but was limited by what was even in those days a tiny memory. (The TX-O was actually just test equipment, designed to support a design project for a much larger computer.) This handicap did have the indirect benefit of removing the machine from the interest and supervision of the Department of Defense, which meant that users whose projects had had too low a priority to qualify for computer time were able to score a few hours. The generally looser atmosphere, and the undeniable fact that the TX-O had not cost the department a fortune, encouraged its guardian, a gentle soul named John MacKenzie, to indulge the railroaders with the occasional unused hour. He opened the door a crack; they burst through like a river at full flood.

One of the first programs they tossed back over their shoulder was a routine that converted Arabic into Roman numerals (by Peter Samson). From a mainframe point of view, a program like this was an absurd waste of time—not Samson's time, no one cared about that, but the computer's time. Run time was so expensive then that the only problems people used computers for were those that humans, who by comparison were practically a free good, were unable to solve on their own. (The usual case being the solution of very long lists of low-level mathematical operations to high levels of accuracy.) As "general purpose" as computers were supposed to be in theory, in real life the experts, who knew the facts about costs, saw very few practical uses for the machines. The internal marketing studies of companies like IBM usually projected total market sizes of a few thousand customers, if that many. While business and technology historians have ridiculed these predictions as failures of corporate vision, they made sense in the context of the time.

The members of the TMRC had a different calculus of practicalities, however. They were émigrés from a world that had systematically, deliberately, cut itself off from thinking about competitive advantages and budget allocations and economic rationality. When the modelers sat down in front of the TX-O they were chasing the same idea they had in the Club itself: to spread wonder and awe, to cook up a few hacks. From that perspective Samson's program looked like the first stroke of a brush across a glistening, virgin canvas. Within weeks the railroaders had commenced a steady flow of games, graphics, the first music synthesis programs (Samson again), and a plenitude of hacks.

The values of the modelers—communal bonhomie, irreverence, high tolerance for goofiness, belief in the power of fantasy, and an insistence on having total control of their own world—were far from the culture of mainstream computing, with its almost theatrical sobriety, high security, to-the-minute metering, and multiple levels of oversight. Conflicts between the two appeared, but never ended as one might have thought, with the modelers being thrown off the TX-O, because overnight they became virtuosos at putting the computer through its paces. Their desire to poke into every corner of the machine, fast-paced information sharing, and high-octane enthusiasm—expressed for instance by hanging around the TX-O virtually 24 hours a day waiting for unused time—gave the modelers a degree of skill light-years beyond those of users constrained by their budgets to plan every keystroke days ahead of time. The modelers used to get time on the machine by offering to do any job that walked in the door in less time than the user had signed up for, in return for the balance. The effect of such unaffected virtuosity on this community can be imagined.

After several months MIT woke up to its new assets and put some of the modelers on the payroll, with their only responsibility being to keep on doing what they were doing. Word of this coven of wizards got out. Digital Equipment Corporation cleverly donated one of the first machines it made to the same lab, correctly anticipating that the modelers would automatically develop volumes of system-enhancing programs. They wrote a long list of useful system tools (programs that allowed the various pieces of hardware to cooperate smoothly), music programs, and tons of games, including a dazzler called "Space Wars" that DEC used for some time as both a diagnostics program and a promotional demo. Jack Dennis wrote a time-sharing program that did for computers what the progressive cab control system had done for model railroads—allow simultaneous operation by many users.

The modelers sometimes called themselves "hackers," which they meant in the traditional sense of pranksters or jesters, people who didn't take life or work too seriously. Soon the rest of the computing world was using the term as well, but in a different sense, to mean "august authority," "voice of overwhelming expertise," or, more demeaningly, "whiz kid." Articles began to appear in newspapers and magazines about MIT's brilliant young cybernauts, announcing that these few youths in Cambridge's Kendall Square were singlehandedly prying open the door to Tomorrowland. (Their nonchalance subliminally strengthened the point; only real geniuses could be so relaxed around *computers*.) Marvin Minsky, the director of MIT's Artificial Intelligence Lab, felt that the episode proved the strong positive relation between individual autonomy and high achievement, and he organized his lab around the principle, hiring a considerable number of the TMRC alumni himself. Years later, in 1984, technology historian Steven Levy wrote a compulsively readable history of the early years of computing, *Hackers*, in which he credited these students with developing an entire sociopolitical ideology of computing, "hackerism," that rippled out to the West Coast and indirectly stimulated the development of the personal computer, in the manner that the encyclopedistes catalyzed the French Revolution.

Building 20, still home to the Club, stands to this day, having managed to outlive the authors of repeated plans to demolish it. One tide running in its favor has been the steady escalation in the costs of disposing of millions of square feet of asbestos tile, though any other university would probably have found the money somewhere. (Harvard recently spent $100,000 in design fees alone disguising a security guardhouse as a very large Bavarian ginger cookie.) The edifice is so ugly (even Freeman would have been appalled) that it is impossible not to admire it, if that makes sense; it has 10 times the righteous nerdly swagger of any other building on campus, and at MIT any building holding that title has a natural constituency.

The Tech Model Railroad Club still has its offices here, and its trains are still controlled by the electromechanical system built from the mid-1950s to the mid-1960s. A mix of industrial-urban and industrial-rural landscapes—factories, warehouses, a lumber mill—rest on a table about four feet high occupying most of what is now a total space of 1200 square feet. There are three main railroad yards, a rail-fed industrial park, an urban transit system, and four settlements (one, Tuckertown, was named after Carleton Tucker), including an urban complex of a dozen city blocks. The atmosphere of the layout seems stuck at about 5 A.M. on Sunday morning. Even in the center of Gifford City (Frank Gifford was another faculty advisor), the largest settlement, where the heights of the buildings would lead you to expect a few spots of bumper-to-bumper traffic, there are just a handful of cars. On my visits the street lamps are usually lit, as if the city lighting utility had stuck to its winter lighting schedule into the spring. The factories and mills scattered across the layout all look buttoned up for the night, if not for a period of serious economic retrenchment.

The fantasy inadvertently comments on the reality, since within the Club itself the pandemonium is gone; the students have drained away, perhaps to the Society for Creative Anachronism, TechSquares, or, more likely, computer games. The club is now the home of a dozen or two middle-aged hobbyists—MIT employees and alumni—of the sort that staff model railroad clubs everywhere else in the world, who come and tinker together on Friday and Saturday nights. The collected volumes of club minutes—almost 50 years worth—run across a shelf in a little side room. Everything is in here: the frowns and smiles levied over the years, the hacks and the spreading of wonder and awe, the painfully acquired expertise on dust and corrosion, the group expeditions to the trains of New Hampshire and to the relay caverns of New England Telephone, the arrival of the catalog from Western Electric and the subsequent shipments of relays, the endless complexities of planning the progressive cab control system; the TX-O. And of course the volumes have their cumulative wisdom as well, for instance that sometimes, if you try to escape the game by dodging into solution space, it just sends the game right in after you. Once when I was examining this shelf of volumes a member passed behind me and said: "We have 10 pounds of trains here and 50 pounds of history." That's not wrong.

SEVEN

The MIT Knee

As with any revolution, the triumph of the engineering sciences brought zealots out to beat the brush (in this case, the corridors) for emblems of the old order whose destruction would serve to illuminate the glory of the new. Inevitably their attention fell upon the courses in mechanical drawing or drafting, which are the arts of using graphics to convey engineering ideas. Not even the most fervent partisan of the subject could claim it was a science, or even had any theory at all worth the name. It was true that the association between mechanical drawing and engineering was as old as Vitruvius or Pythagoras, that the subject had been near the core of the curriculum from the Institute's first day, that the tools of the trade—the protractor and right-edge, parallel edges, the colored pens, the sheets of cutout patterns—had grown into as reliable a symbol of the profession among the general public as the slide rule, and that most engineers still required some grasp of the vocabulary. But in an atmosphere that came close to believing that any feature of the profession more than five years old was ipso facto archaic, badges of merit, a distinguished history, and venerable position carried with them more vulnerability than protection.

The head of the Engineering Design and Graphics Division in the mid-1950s, a professor named John Arnold, countered this political threat by changing the meaning of design from "the language used to tell fabrication and assembly where to make their cuts" into the language of innovation, the format in which the engineering imagination expressed itself. For a hundred years mechanical drawing had been taught by herding the students through a succession of standardized exercises requiring the representation of conventional machine elements (like pistons or flanges). Arnold commenced his course with a dramatic description of a planet totally unlike Earth, in which the atmosphere was (for example) natural gas and the gravitational field 20 times stronger than Earth's, or weaker, or there was no rain, or it rained all the time and the inhabitants were fish. The plants grew with their roots in the atmosphere and their fruits underground. People had eyes in the back of their heads and four legs and needed to eat every 10 minutes. After Arnold had built up the details of an environment in which everything was new, alien, and disorienting, he would assign design tasks: a bus, a plough, an elevator, and so on, each expected to show a sensitivity to the details of the alien environment.

Arnold's new course was a brilliant save, capturing as it did the futuristic spirit of the engineering sciences even in the absence of theoretical abstractions. (Many of the plans developed by his students were so striking and elegant, so in tune with the moment, that they were exhibited around the Institute as art.) Nonetheless, not all the members of the faculty felt completely comfortable training their undergraduates to, as they saw it, illustrate the covers of science fiction magazines. In 1957 Arnold decided he had been passed over for promotion once too often and left for a university more sympathetic to the Arcturan approach (Stanford). His position as the head of the Design Center, together with the responsibility for dealing with the Center's political vulnerability, was handed on to a junior member of the faculty, Bob Mann.

Mann was in some respects a throwback to the people who originally enrolled in MIT just after the Civil War: experienced engineers with an established career history. He had grown up in a tough corner of Brooklyn where no one gave college a thought (neither of his parents had even attended high school), gone to a vocational high school, and upon graduation had proceeded straight into industry. Eventually, after being drafted and demobilized, he found himself in a company with an academic work culture (AT&T), where he was persuaded to draw upon his GI Bill credits and go back to school. He enrolled at MIT because the name had the strongest associations with engineering.

Mann's class photo, taken in 1950, shows a head with flaring eyebrows, ears standing away from the skull, as if half-cupped to the viewer, full lips, and a significant nose. His hair is already beginning to thin. Unlike the subjects of the other photos on the page, Mann does not seem to be sitting down: his head and shoulders are tilted across the plane of the photo, as if he were throwing a glance in the direction of the camera while striding by in a rush. You half expect to see his tie flying back over his shoulder. His focus is not aimed in the zone around the camera lens, where yearbook photographers tell their subjects to look, but off behind the viewer's right shoulder. The muscles of his face are so gathered, the expression so intense, serious, and interested, that one has to fight an impulse to turn around and follow his gaze. During his undergraduate years he discovered an unsuspected talent for politics, at least for the frat-versus-prole version that dominated student life, leading the proles in a half-dozen campus organizations, including the Catholic Club. In his senior year he was elected president of his class.

Mann had come out of and expected to return to industrial engineering; from that point of view MIT was basically a pit stop. During his junior year he married a physicist with ties to the Institute, however, so he stayed on, first as a graduate student, and a few years after that as an assistant professor in Mechanical Engineering, a fate that back in Brooklyn would have seemed as probable as a career in finger painting. When the appointment to Design and Graphics fell his way he had no clear idea where to take the division. He knew he wasn't going to be doing any extraterrestrial engineering; on the other hand, returning to the prewar mechanical drawing curriculum was politically impossible and intellectually unappealing. Arnold's basic idea—redefining design as the expression of the engineering imagination—was clearly right for the times; the only question was the right context for that imagination. Mann started thinking in various directions, and then, in one of those miracles of synchronicity that sometimes arise, found John Kenneth Dupress knocking at his door.

Dupress was a go-ahead character who had compensated for horrific war injuries—the loss of his sight and his right hand—with a passionate interest in finding technological solutions for the problems of the handicapped. He had thought up dozens of candidate innovations himself, and was especially enthusiastic about a device he called a mobility aid, a cane that would sense the distance from its point to the nearest surface and communicate that number to the user through vibrations. The mobility aid was a challenging project, but Dupress had a long list of simpler ideas: There wasn't even an English-to-Braille typewriter on the market. The collapsible canes then available were junk (the sleeves wore out in weeks). He had chased down Mann as part of a tour through institutions he associated with technological innovation, buttonholing professors about his enthusiasms, trying to strike a spark.

Mann saw that tools for the handicapped made a perfect replacement for Arnold's extraterrestrial applications. They represented real needs of real people, the absence of which had given the previous curriculum such a strange taste. If a design had exceptional merit there were established societies and agencies that could be approached for development grants. The list of needs, of possible kinds of tools, was bottomless: each handicapped person faced a set of life tasks that were not only different from those of the able-bodied but from most others with the same handicap (the correct wheelchair design for a paraplegic might well be decided by the floor plan of the user's apartment). Mann started assigning projects from Dupress's list and working up new ideas to add to them. Unlike the courses of the past, including Arnold's courses, some of the designs were actually built in real hardware as opposed to drawn on paper, including the English-to-Braille typewriter, a video text enlarger for the vision impaired, a Braille translator for compositor tape, and a number of devices to support physical therapy exercises and routines.

Building physically real devices and using real people to test them reintroduced the unpredictability and chaos that is the hallmark of real solution space. One time a student decided to design and build a basketball for the blind—a ball whose trajectories could be defined through sound localization. The trick was to make the ball acoustically pointlike, so that a player trying to catch a ball coming from any arbitrary angle and at any speed (within reason) could define its center quickly enough to move his or her hands into the right position. Meeting that specification required—among other fine points—distributing sound-emitting apertures evenly around the sphere while keeping the weight of the device close to that of a normal basketball. After months a working version of the ball, by then a technical marvel on several counts, was taken to the Perkins School for the Blind in nearby Watertown, Massachusetts, where the children played with it politely for several minutes before handing it back and returning to their usual games.

On the other hand, as the law of unpredictability would have predicted, some projects succeeded beyond any reasonable hope. One day Mann got a call from an orthopedic surgeon. A patient of his, an MIT professor, had been talking about controlling prostheses with thought, just the way natural muscles were. Was this true? Was this possible?

The professor in question was Norbert Wiener, a mathematician and polymath's polymath. Wiener read voraciously in 13 languages and not only remembered what he read but thought about it to startling effect, often finding depths of implication that the original author had not begun to grasp. He was one of the first scientists to understand natural processes in terms of information flow as opposed to simple kinetics; to think of the universe and its parts as in perpetual conversation, as he was with his colleagues, linked by a complex of intertwined feedback loops and knots. Wiener saw the loss of a limb or extremity less as the loss of bodily function than of a sensory modality from which the brain learned how the body and the world were getting on together. He had had many conversations with Mann about restoring this flow of information by embedding sensors in artificial limbs and electrodes in stumps. Prostheses fascinated him as one of the best ways to explore this information loop: "The way to learn about watches is to repair them," he would say. Though ostensibly on the mathematics faculty, Wiener spent a good deal of time working on a device intended to allow the deaf to monitor the distribution of frequencies in their own voice (as an aid to learning speech) through mechanical vibrators on the skin.

Wiener was a compulsive monologist. "How are you," he would say on being introduced, adding without pausing for a second, "Let me tell you what I've been thinking about." And he would be off on one of perhaps sixty themes of constant interest. Undergraduates, lost tourists, secretaries, parents inspecting the campus with their aspiring children, delivery workers, campus police, anyone at all might turn about and find this plump, goateed professor standing splayfooted at their side sharing some remarkable, or maybe just incomprehensible, new connection or feat of analysis that had just flowered in his mind. In the early 1960s Wiener broke his hip and went into a hospital, where he continued his habits of torrential and inspirational discourse. His surgeon staggered out of his own baptism in this flow convinced that what had seemed the fantastic possibility of controlling an artificial arm with nerve signals was at the point of practicality. Mann's name had rushed by in the monologue, and the physician was calling to find out where and when he could place his order.

The problem above-the-elbow prostheses had to address was that their users had one convenient source of control signals—hunching the shoulder up or down—and two control problems—flexing the (artificial) elbow joint and operating the spring-loaded clamper usually attached to the wrist. While in theory shrug sequence could be encoded into commands of any desired complexity, amputees had always found the effort more trouble than it was worth. Prosthetics engineers had tried taping control switches over muscle groups and training amputees to throw those switches by bulging or hardening them in some way. Nothing acceptable had turned up there, either.

Wiener's idea was to tape electrodes over the biceps and triceps, the muscles used naturally to flex and straighten the elbow, and monitor them for electrical activity. An electrical pulse running to the biceps would turn the motor in the prosthesis on and send it running in the "flex" direction; a pulse to the triceps would reverse it. (The clasper would continue to be controlled from the shoulder.) Such a system would require no training, because the artificial elbow would be responding to the same commands as the original. It would mean building a machine that could, after a fashion, read minds, but why not? Mann loved the idea. "I knew nothing about biology, neurophysiology, any of that," he remembers happily. "I was just a classical engineer, jumping into a project."

A classical engineer—this is part of the concept—knows when to make special preparations, and Mann brought a new tool on board for this expedition: one of the first simulators. At this time, the mid-1960s, computers were just beginning to become accessible to a few engineers, and Mann, whose contacts in that industry were unbeatable (his roommate during his undergraduate years had been Ken Olsen of Digital Equipment Corporation), was one of those few. One of the core problems of the project was that while the location of the nerves carrying the elbow control signals was known, their syntax—how a nerve instruction that told an elbow to fold at a rate of perhaps one inch a second differed from one telling the same joint to snap shut—was not. While nobody expected an artificial elbow to achieve the precision of response of a natural joint, obviously there had to be some match between the expectation of the user and the behavior of the prosthesis. Arriving at this agreement would be impossible unless the language the brain and body used for their conversations could be translated.

Mann wrote an animation program that moved a graphic representation of a prosthesis into different orientations at different speeds, depending on the values chosen for variables like motor strength, weight distribution, and length. Once this device was working he taped sensors on the upper arm muscles of fully able volunteers, connected those leads to his simulator, and asked the subjects to open and close their elbows at an average, comfortable rate. Different values were then entered into the design formulas until the arm of the human subject and the arm in the animation were moving synchronously. When they were, that was evidence that the particular constellation of design values plugged into the simulator was biologically reasonable—that a rough translation of the meaning of the nerve signals had been made.

For these design variables (of course they were not the only open questions) the simulator sped up the cycles of generate-and-test, gave more possibilities their innings, and threw those particular corners of solution space into higher resolution. The product that emerged was extraordinarily successful: After only three years of development the Boston Arm was spun off to a private company. (It even proved possible to use muscle signals for graded control, to control the rate of flexing with thought. Nerve-signal control has since been extended to artificial wrists, though fingers remain out of reach.)

The obvious next step was to extend these ideas to the design of an artificial knee: the market was enormous (above-the-knee amputations are one sequela of diabetes), and the A/K prostheses then available had not been especially well received. On the other hand, while knee motion might appear even simpler than elbow motion, it is not. Unlike elbows, knees do not work in isolation, one at a time; they work in pairs, as a synchronized team (except for hopping), handing a common stride length and pace rate back and forth, from one partner to the other. Over their lifetimes these two partners generate dozens, hundreds of these dances, depending on speed, terrain, age, weight and distribution of weight, personality, shoes, and mood. A woman shuffling forward in a crowd is exchanging a very different set of signals with her knees than when she is rushing to make an appointment, wandering through a garden or through sand or over an icy sidewalk, climbing stairs, dancing, or carrying a bag of groceries. To a skilled eye, everyone walking down the street has a different gait: people strut, mince, speedwalk, stroll, swagger, glide, bounce, stagger, roll, and creep along. (It is even possible that we use these differences to recognize ourselves. Neuropsychologist Oliver Sachs has described a syndrome in which a leg seems to have been removed and the limb of some stranger attached in its place. The etiology of this sensation is still unclear, but one possibility is that its victims have lost control of their gait. Perhaps occasionally a clocking neuron somewhere in the central nervous system lets go, allowing some critical reports to arrive a second off the beat, and when that happens we feel our flesh transform into a stranger's.)

One of the more crucial synchronization issues is the rate of weight shifting—the rhythm of those moments when the body mass is lifted off one leg and balanced on the other so the first can swing forward. Each of these various gaits possesses its own rate of shifting, and both knees must be tuned to the same rate if the user is not to fall over. A conventional A/K prosthesis design, which is fundamentally a peg-leg with a hinge, swings at only one speed, that of a natural pendulum of that length. A user trying to walk slower or faster than this frequency of the lower limb would arrive at the point of weight shift "before" the limb did—before (or after) the moment of maximum extension had been reached— which would make it impossible to complete the stride without disrupting the pace. Thus amputees were constrained to one gait only, regardless of the circumstances.

Building a leg that could switch among a family of gaits might require one or more motors and brakes, some kind of energy conservation device (like tendons in real legs), dozens of extremely intricate sequences of control instructions for those brakes and motors, and some system for recognizing which sequence was appropriate when. All these systems had to be enormously reliable (a leg that periodically dumped its users on the street was unthinkable), while running in an operating environment in which the full body weight of the user dropped down like a hammer blow with each weight shift. The whole package had to be cosmetically realistic and not weigh more than 40 pounds at the very most. Solving some of these problems would be easier than expected (possibly the motions of the natural leg might be used to write and select the control schemes), but some would be harder. A prudent estimate of the amount of working time involved might run to man-centuries.

Finally, it was by no means certain that there was a market for the device. In general the handicapped have a bias toward simple, solid, low-tech prostheses whose reliability is guaranteed by self-evident simplicity, and this prejudice is particularly intense with respect to tools intended to carry them into traffic (A/K prostheses had hardly changed at all since World War I, and not all that much since the Civil War). The complaint most A/K amputees make about these prostheses now is not the lack of gait variety but the inadequacy of the socket that attaches the leg to their stump: that it gets sweaty and chafes the skin and falls out of adjustment. Presumably they felt the same way then. (Elderly users also dislike how much raw human energy it takes to walk with a prosthesis. No doubt some of that cost is attributable to the inflexibility of gait, but probably not all.) A gait-versatile prosthesis might well turn out to be very comfortable and popular in practice—and possibly other improvements might be added at the same time, like a powered knee that could lift weight—but certainly nobody was demonstrating in the streets demanding one.

In short, the resources available to develop an artificial multigait knee as a real product were a tiny fraction of those likely to be necessary. Had Mann been working in the pre-war Institute or a proprietary development company the project would have died immediately. But by the late 1960s he had another option: letting it bubble up to graduate school; redefining it from a question of design (actually building a multigait knee) to one of engineering science (finding the information needed to build one later).

One of the first students to work on the problem bore the memorable name Woodie Flowers, the same student who had worked on the basketball for the blind. Flowers devoted his Ph.D. to the design of an artificial knee simulator—a heavily instrumented prosthesis connected by cables to a minicomputer and a hydraulic power system (sitting on two large carts) that could be set to drive the knee through a range of stride length and timing settings. The subject, often Flowers himself, would strap the leg on and walk around within the limits of his tether, describing how different settings felt. "I kept dreaming about legs that would learn," Flowers says now. "All during the day they'd try to get better and better. Then at the end of the day the person would vote on how his leg behaved." This dream was of course about Flowers himself, sitting by his control console, imagining himself in the knee, a leg that was learning, struggling to do better, waiting for verdicts from his subject.

Among other questions, this instrument was used to explore the nature of the power needed to reproduce the performance curves of biological knees. In theory a pendulum can be forced to move at a speed different from its natural frequency by exerting power or applying braking. It seemed intuitively obvious that the knee did both, but the point was not certain and the issue was critical, since weight constraints dictated that only the lightest, and therefore the weakest, batteries could possibly be onboard. Finding and describing which mixtures of active and passive power (motors and brakes) could simulate the behavior of real knees was an independent issue of intrinsic interest, and not just to prosthetic engineers: biologists, roboticists, and even animators might find use for the result.

Flowers's experiments showed that most of the important gait changes (like the difference between how knees operate when walking faster or slower) could be reproduced entirely with passive power, using brakes to shape the forces passed down from the hip. A knee with no motors had limitations—it couldn't do deep knee bends or play sports or lift its user up a flight of stairs—but it could generate lots of gaits, if not every possible one. The bad news was that the nerve signals in the thigh controlling the knee were more complex than in the case of the upper arm and were muffled by thick layers of overlying fat.

Amputations usually left the nerve geometry in ruins as well. A multigait knee needs to know at least two pieces of information: what kind of gait the body wants to be in (how fast it wants to walk and how long a stride it wants to take) and which phase of the walking cycle (weight shift, heel lift-off, swing forward, strike downward, weight bearing) comes next. Neither of these pieces of information was likely to be learned from listening to the nerves, at least not in the short run.

Between 1973 and 1990 almost 50 theses joined Flowers's in the Engineering Library on topics like the gait dynamics of amputees, the details of gait phases, the nature of gait shifting, the properties of muscles in a stump, the specifications that various parts, brakes, motors, controllers, and sensors would have to meet, and so on. (The NSF, which had been funding work on the multiple gait knee since 1971, kept extending the grant; the total amount spent over all these years was about half a million.) The problem of teaching the gait and phase information to the knee kept growing more complex. For a few years there was hope of placing motion sensors on the normal leg and then shifting their reports a half-beat backward or forward in time. The idea worked technically, but nobody could find a scheme for attaching the motion sensors that amputees could tolerate. Some students ventured out into unexplored corners such as wheeled prostheses, which of course had no troublesome gait or phase. Eventually some research suggested that the fine details of the rolling contact made by the foot with the floor, especially the structure of pressure changes radiating across the heel as it lifts off the ground, gave good leverage on both questions. It was not clear how a working prosthesis would acquire this information (an instrumented shoe inlay, like an orthopedic pad, would get beaten into junk in days), but it was clear which way solution space was pointing.

By the mid-1980s the implosion of electronics parts had shrunk the electronics required to manipulate the sensor and control software to the size of a pack of gum, and a real artificial multigait knee finally began to seem practical. Assembling one would be a huge job, especially since the only credit a student could expect for straight engineering (as opposed to producing more engineering science theory) was a master's degree at best. Still, it was possible that the project could be divided into more than one master's or (more likely) that some undergraduates could be hired to assist. Mike Goldfarb, a graduating senior from the University of Arizona, came by during his round of preapplication interviews in 1989, expressed strong interest, and was admitted. That summer, Flowers (who had joined the MIT faculty) called Goldfarb and told him that the NSF had canceled the contract. The NSF only funds research and, not entirely unreasonably, viewed putting an actual knee together as development; the Veterans Administration did fund development, but until a working model of the knee had been made and tested there was in their view nothing to develop. Goldfarb was on an independent fellowship, so his tuition money was safe, but he'd be working alone and unable to buy much. He said he'd come anyway.

Mike Goldfarb is short and slight, with a shy, diffident manner. His light brown hair juts out like a shelf over a tall, thin face that narrows forward into a wedge. In the fall of 1990 he often wore an orange turtleneck with tan corduroys. When he is called upon to speak, for instance to answer a question, he tends to start and stop the first sentence five or six times in a quiet, soft voice, as if translating into some language he knows imperfectly. "I don't see . . . Hmm . . . But then we don't . . . Humph . . . Well, to be perfectly precise . . . " The thick eyebrows over his hazel eyes are constantly popping up and down. Some psychologists claims this clocks the pace of the cognitions streaming just behind them.

Goldfarb says he was leaning toward prosthetic engineering even in his undergraduate years, when he worked summers at a VA hospital. Part of what drew him in that direction was "working with the best," by which he means not his colleagues in the profession but natural selection, the engineer responsible for biological structure. A person building a design that the body is willing to accept as part of its apparatus, even grudgingly, is like a chessplayer getting a kind word from Gari Kasparov. The field also draws the engineer into a direct relationship with the raw subjectivities, the unquantifiable likes and dislikes, of the people expected to use the tools being designed, a rare privilege in a culture where priority of access usually goes to marketing.

Visitors sometimes wonder what lies on the other side of the abstracted look so often remarked of MIT students, and here is one known case: In the first months after he arrived, as he walked up the Infinite Corridor or across the campus, Goldfarb was thinking his way down into his knees, focusing on their life, feeling them lift up, swing forward, strike downward. He imagined them as Wiener would have, as communicating entities. He tried to think through what they could know of the world, what they were in a position to tell the brain, and what sort of directives they could accept and respect from command central. Sometimes he walked from the point of view of the body, feeling himself drop and lift and drop on the leg like a flesh piledriver; at other times he would play catcher and imagine being the leg, receiving the blows like a nail under a hammer. He walked for days as if he were an amputee himself, pulling his body up stairs with a single knee or with one ankle locked. Often when he walked he would picture his whole body linkage moving, like a wire-frame skeleton in space, the rhythms of mechanical force radiating down from the hip and up from the floor.

For the first several months he hardly touched a piece of hardware, spending his time sitting in the library, working on a model of the energy cycle of the normal knee. As mentioned above, ordinary prostheses are exhausting to use, and the engineer wanted to build the most energy-efficient linkage he could. No text can touch nature for excellence of design in wringing the most work from the fewest calories, as anyone who has tried to lose weight through exercise knows all too well. Goldfarb was looking for tips, figuring out the optimums, setting the bar, fixing a target. Every so often Flowers would come by and give him a nudge.

Eventually he started, weaving together the terms and measures of kinetics (the distribution and transformation of mechanical force), dynamics (making or absorbing force), circuit design, information theory or signal processing, programming, clinical issues (reliability, safety, and comfort), cost of manufacture, an encyclopedic command of the parts catalogs, and—every project has its unique demands—the ability to scrounge. Goldfarb would go to rehabilitation and power electronics conferences, target a vendor, hang out with its exhibitors, and fire them up about some aspect of the project (the challenge of it all, the potential market of 2 million people). Back at MIT, he would wait a few days for them to have mentioned the project to their higher-ups and then pop them for a donation. He developed begging to such an art that he started cadging parts that cost $50 or $75; Flowers had to remind Goldfarb that they weren't that poor.

That was only one level of assembly; a second could be described less abstractly, in terms of instruction statements and magnetic brakes and sensors, the physical, detailed world of soldering and programming and nuts and bolts. A third, more general, was the integration of the last 20 years of this project itself: the dozens of theses, now scattered around Goldfarb's desk, the hundreds of hours that students had spent thumping around the floor in Flowers's simulator, Wiener's vision of the mind-body loop as a complex of feed-backs, and even a bit of John Kenneth Dupress, whose enthusiasms were still faintly there, glowing in the Lab for Biomechanics and Human Rehabilitation like microwave radiation left over from the Big Bang. These were all folded in and connected up.

By the fall of 1990 any visitor to the Institute could have watched Goldfarb tinkering with what was clearly, strik-ingly, a leg. It seemed destined less for humans than for a cyborg or robot, the rest of which one half expected to see sitting in a waiting room around the corner, scrolling through old geographic databases. The foot of the MIT knee is a lemony beige, formed from a block of fine plastic foam into the general dimensions of a foot with unformed toes. An aluminum tube, an artificial shin an inch thick and eight inches long (the house where the sensors live), connects the foot to a long, black matte metal cage, inside which sits a bronze-capped metal cup the size of a tulip bulb. That season the leg lay on an ancient wooden bench, so scarred and scuffed it might have been recycled from the old Dynamo Lab, which once embraced this space.

Usually when I looked in Goldfarb was trying to force the software into errors, feeding bizarre thoughts into the knee's computer, trying to trap it into doing something interesting or iconoclastic, which is of course not what one wants from a knee. He had begged a processor simulator from NEC that allowed him to watch the operation of the computer on a level of detail that was the equivalent in physiological terms of watching a thought wind through a brain, neuron by neuron. Once I observed absently that this must be a fun project, which was in truth a pretty banal remark: There had been 20 years of sowing out there and Goldfarb was the one who got to reap. Of course it was fun. "It's neat," Goldfarb agreed soberly. Something in his tone made me look up. His brown eyes were dancing and his lips were trembling. For about a tenth of a second the lab was lit with a sunburst of sheer animal glee. Then it was gone. "Very neat," he repeated, gathering his sobriety back around him again.

EIGHT

The Media Lab

The fires of radicalism that blew around the globe in the last third of the 1960s struck sparks in every corner. Even in ordinarily fireproof professions like law and medicine, apoplectic elders found the parables of service that had nurtured professional fee schedules for hundreds of years recast into tales of elitist oppression and exploitation. These histories all had the same deep structure: beginning with an age in which the skills of the profession were the common property of all, and ending with the tragedy of feudal and capitalist class consciousness stripping the people of control over their lives and charging them for it to boot. The variant in architecture, for instance, was that since the birth of the species its members had been free to build and rebuild their structures whenever they liked (hunter-gatherers could always build a new hut). Then, over the last thousand years, this natural harmony between humans and their shelter had been destroyed by a hierarchical elite of commodity fetishists and their lackey specialist sidekicks: the architects.

For young architects, the agenda imposed by this history of injustice was to dedicate their career, or at least part of it, to returning "the power to control their own space" to the people. Even at a relatively apolitical university like MIT a group of architect/engineers (funded by the Ford Foundation!) was trying to develop software that would guide untrained novices through all the complexities of contemporary building design, from building codes to light exposure. The vision that animated the group and its director, a charismatic young architect named Nicholas Negroponte, was that of a person or family or group of families, perhaps living in some public development atrocity, sitting together and using this program to design their own house directly, without professional mediation. Ideally, they wouldn't even need contractors. If the building materials were intelligent and flexible enough, the house could shift into its new design automatically, perhaps while the family was at the movies.

Conventionally minded architects—architects over 30—found this concept of an "architecture machine" unintuitive, partly because they found it hard to imagine how the specific materials, the wires and pipes and structural elements, would go about reconfiguring themselves. Such materials were of course a very long way from development, so Negroponte devised the idea of displaying the key elements of the concept in a metaphorical context. He had his group construct a mechanical arm that stacked and restacked piles of one-inch cubes into columns of different heights. This arm worked systematically but at random, compiling and retaining in memory a list of the locations of every accessible cube, choosing one from the list at random, and then moving it to some other site, also picked at random.

When the arm was finished Negroponte covered the surface with a glass cage and released a colony of gerbils into it. As the gerbils ran around they interacted with the cubes, pushing them into new orientations, toppling columns over, and so forth. Each time the arm reached for a cube but found it missing, it noted that fact by lowering the likelihood of moving any other cube in the cage that was defined as having the same kind of relation to its neighborhood. (If columns four cubes high tended to be knocked over, then the arm would build fewer four-cube stacks.) In a sense, Negroponte argued, the machine was accepting design decisions from the gerbils and reshaping their environment in accordance with those decisions, just the way a real architecture machine would.

In late 1970 Negroponte brought the gerbil architecture machine to New York City, where the Jewish Museum had organized a show on art and "contemporary control and communication techniques." A number of distinguished contemporary artists had work on view: John Baldessari cremated some paintings in a mortuary and interred the ashes in the walls of the museum; Les Levine exhibited videotapes recorded in his studio "showing the artist in his natural environment." Surprisingly, given the competition, the piece from MIT dominated the show. Every story in the media mentioned it, usually prominently, and the museum chose the machine for the cover of the show catalog as the most emblematic progeny of the marriage of art and information technology.

The reviews suggest that not every New Yorker actually caught the architecture machine concept; what they seemed to see instead was a compelling vision of life in the computerized future, a world in which a huge gantry arm would swing over New York, pick up apartments and co-ops, and drop them randomly around town. Any morning you might wake up and find your property sitting in the Bronx. You would have no idea of your net worth or personal security from one day to the next. The exhibit yanked the feelings people had (and still have) about computers and the forces of science, life in New York, progress, and the thrills of riding the tides of supply and demand right up out of the preconscious.

When the arm picked up a cube it would first drop it down an orientation chute to straighten out the corners, tapping it a little if the cube jammed. Sometimes the arm would capture a bit of gerbil tail when it picked up a cube, snatch the astonished little rodent up in the air, swing it over the chute and drop it. Because the rodent was hanging by its tail underneath the cube, first the gerbil would fall into the chute and then the cube would land on it from above; as the rodent tried to climb up out of the chute, which was too narrow for it to fall through, the arm would tap on its head from above, trying to push it back down. It was so New York.

The Architecture Machine Group (or, as it was known locally, Arc Mac) had a number of other interests, and the success of the museum show encouraged the Group to illustrate them with the same kind of allusive, indirect metaphor. One example was intended to illustrate the potential of identifying information with nontextual attributes like color, spatial location, and symbolic graphics. During the 1970s a number of software engineers, most prominently a group at Xerox PARC on the West Coast, were pointing out that a person reaching for aspirin in a cabinet or a paper on a desk or a book in a bookcase usually relies less on text as presented by labels or covers than cues like color, height, and shelf position. Perhaps the same techniques would be useful in organizing, filing, and providing access to files in a computer. (Eventually the engineers at Xerox gave a tour to a youth named Steve Jobs, who designed the Macintosh computer around their ideas.) Still, the practicality of associating computer files with colors, positions, sizes, and icons, as opposed to filenames organized in sorted lists, was not clear to everyone (nor is it yet).

So in the mid-1970s Negroponte built an elegant office with recessed lighting and rich brown furnishings (except for one wall apparently of frosted glass) with an Eames chair in the center. "This is the Media Room," a visitor would be told, "and this . . . " whereupon the wall of glass, 13 feet on the diagonal, would fill with portraits, maps, little display screens, letters, book covers, a calendar . . . "is Dataland!" Two tiny joysticks were set into the arms of the chair; move one to the left, and the symbols on the screen would flow to the right, giving the impression of steering over the landscape. In seconds you would be skimming "cities and neighborhoods of information" (less lyrically, clusters of symbols), hovering over fields of faces (each representing a file of correspondence), arrays of book symbols, meadows of maps.

Dataland, which Negroponte liked to call an "informational surround," was in no sense a real-world, finished product. The wall-sized TV display was actually a rear-projection thrown from a room behind the screen, and obviously no display system requiring a room's worth of floor space was remotely practical. There was no real-world data in the machine, nothing reflecting any experience with how the concept might play out in a genuine office. Dataland was a "sketch-in-hardware" of one way graphics might be used to manage files and data once the idea had proved itself and all the engineering problems had been solved. To many engineers, including many members of the MIT faculty, a device with so many ifs was just so much fantasy, but there were other constituencies to whom these caveats were un-important. Foremost among these were the video media, who were forever on the prowl for new ways of capturing the futuristic buzz in visual terms.

As word about the Group spread, Arc Mac developed extensive contacts with the worldwide community of "future groupies," persons whose job and passion are to know where tomorrow is happening today. Sometimes the members of this polyglot tribe (Japanese architects, Canadian newspaper editors, scouts for Dutch venture capital, high-tech newsletter editors and other science media factotums, technology stock analysts up from New York, Silicon Valley VPs for corporate R&D, think tankers, strategic marketing consultants, science fiction writers and editors, science educators, documentary producers, technology artists, science museum exhibit designers) gave the impression they thought Arc Mac was MIT. They would get out of their cabs in Kendall Square and stumble around the corridors, bouncing in and out of the Departments of Chemical Engineering and Materials Science, the Research Lab for Electronics, and the Lab for Computer Science, and in each of these places, presumably just as focused on "the future" as Arc Mac, they would look around for a receptionist and ask for directions to the Machine Group, as though the rest of the institution was so much white noise.

Certainly no other corner at MIT boasted the equivalent of the Aspen "Movie Map," in which a person could sit down in the Eames chair and actually drive through the streets of downtown Aspen (a computer would note which way the joysticks were moved, pull the appropriate images off a videodisk, and project them on the wall display). A critic might argue that there was no obvious function, no community of demand, calling for simulating a drive through the center of a city, and even if there had been, image storage technology was not remotely adequate to support the level of performance implied by the Aspen demo. (The military, which picked up much of the funding, thought Movie Maps might be used to train tank drivers to get around in foreign cities.)

While Negroponte obviously did not go out of his way to impress the limitations of the demo on his visitors, my guess is that neither point would have slowed the flow of groupie traffic. The Aspen demo connected to something much deeper than these details: the coalescing state of mind that would eventually be known as cocooning; the impulse to withdraw from society, to seal oneself off, to not be touched. The idea that somebody at MIT had figured out how to fix it so you didn't have to leave your home to drive downtown hit the center of the culture to within a millimeter's precision. What makes great science fiction is not prescience but an ability to speak to the present, allusively but exactly. The sense of breathing some kind of superoxygen wafting down from the future became most intense when the Arc Mac closed this connection.

Negroponte wrapped these demos up into a narrative about the future of "the human interface," "the physical, sensory, and intellectual space that lies between computers and ourselves." He distinguished between interfaces that were "unfamiliar, cold, and unwelcoming" and those that were like places "we know and love, those that are familiar, comfortable, warm, and, most important, personal." The point of Arc Mac was to demonstrate the ways in which interfaces of the second kind might look and work. The interface theme suggested a revolution in the feel of the world, the opening of a new frontier to be settled and developed by those smart enough to get their minds in gear and their money down early, and a huge market embracing every industrial sector, since by definition all computers (and for that matter, all tools) had interfaces that could be made warmer and more personal. While spelling out the exact meaning and consequences of this distinction was admittedly not easy, purely as a high concept it certainly sounded like the right idea.

The demos legitimized the interface by showing it was more than talk, and the interface legitimized the demos by pulling them into a coherent, mutually reinforcing set of themes. When Negroponte talked in Japan or Paris or San Francisco the audience saw not another stem-winding futurist, which are two for a dollar, but a person who was insuring his predictions by making them happen. He began to raise money from an extraordinary range of industrial sectors: financial services, automotive, TV, chemicals, computers, movies, publishing, photography, broadcasting, even toys (Lego of Denmark). By 1985 he was able to expand Arc Mac, now renamed The Media Lab, to the point where it occupied most of a new building on the eastern edge of the campus. (A prerogative earned by raising a large share of the money for the building.)

Though formally named after an MIT president, Jerome Weisner, the building started to be called after the Lab almost immediately, in part because its look harmonized so well with that of the Media Lab itself. The Weisner is a boxy, sleek, virtually windowless, five-story affair covered with a grid of large white metal tiles. Pulses of color are inscribed between the tiles, and these give it a flickering, edgy, electronic feeling. "The squareness of the box and the smoothness of the skin make the building appear self-contained and sealed off from the life of the world around it, like a Christmas present that has yet to be unwrapped," an architect wrote in a review. A huge atrium soars from the ground to

the roof, a triumph of art over utility that could hardly go
unmarked in a community where the demand for working
floor space is so consuming and unceasing. *The New York
Times Sunday Magazine* did a story, as did *Time, Fortune,*
and most of the general science and technology media. (Both
the *Times* and Brand gave their overviews the sweeping title
"Inventing the Future".)

The Lab funds itself through "sponsorships," which
include reports, presentations, consultations, visiting scientist arrangements, and, of course, the right to see all the
demos. They are sold to product and marketing executives
(as opposed to people responsible for manufacturing, a more
traditional MIT audience), with the idea of providing useful
examples of where technology might go, what it might look
like, 5 or 10 or even 15 years from now. While directed
research arrangements—concentration on specific questions—can be had, the basic market strategy is to keep the
price of participation low, $25,000 a year, or about the price
of a high-end newsletter, and the numbers of sponsors high
(six or seven dozen).

Over the last few years these funds have paid for dozens
of demos, including videos of a "desktop secretary" negoti-
ating appointments, making reservations, checking for
schedule changes, listening for reports on traffic conditions
on the road to the airport, dunning subordinates for tardy
memos, and summoning taxis at the end of the day; lip-
reading computers; a music synthesizer that can accept a
musical score, listen to a human performance, and then
generate a supporting accompaniment appropriate to the
interpretation of that artist; and a display terminal that
tracks the users' eyes and can dilate, either graphically or
with text, on whichever point of the graphical landscape the
user's gaze might linger. (A casual browser pursuing a catalog based on this technology would see nothing but images;

but the moment one caught his eye the document would begin to extol the pleasures awaiting those wise enough to purchase the particular item, while rotating the product through attractive perspectives.)

One rainy day I was driven through Cambridge on a demo of "Back Seat Driver," an automated navigator that was supposed to figure out which turns the driver should make to get to any specified destination and pass this advice on through a speech synthesizer. (The program got hopelessly, endearingly, confused.) Perhaps the most common demo, at least in the early years of the Lab, was a demonstration of how newspaper readers might use computers to augment stories with biographical or cartographical databases, or organize inches of display according to how much interest was expressed in previous stories of that sort, or mix items drawn from their appointment book into the news of the day. Again, none of these demos represented real products, or even products for which there was articulated, preexisting demand. (The information services required for an interactive news display are nowhere near the market.) They were like coming attractions trailers, only for technologies.

The most widely viewed demos hang on the glass walls of the Spatial Imaging Project (SIP), the group at the Media Lab looking into holography. These images (a still life of metallic fruits, an X-ray of a brain, a portrait of Leonardo, and an image of a sports car) have been impressed on transparent film using a special technique that makes them visible only to viewers whose gaze is directly perpendicular to the image. Walking up to the wall you see nothing until the moment of closest approach, when the hologram explodes out of your peripheral vision with a vividness that feels like a pop in the face. The effect is that of an art gallery peeking out from some alternate dimension, loosing four quick blasts of graphics, and then twitching back into invisibility. It could not feel more satisfyingly *tomorrow*.

When holograms first appeared in the 1960s the general expectation was that 3-D television was at most a few years away. "Anybody could start up a company with 'Holo' in the title, make two or three phone calls, and get $3 million," the director of SIP, Steve Benton, remembers. The triumph of the new medium seemed so inevitable that the New York cognoscenti even prepared a hologram museum to receive the new art form. Unfortunately, the engineers assigned to travel through the curtain of hype and actually bring the technology to market returned with bad news. Holography works, or does not, according to its success at filtering out and recording the differences between the way a scene looks to our right and left eye. These differences are subtle, barely at the edge of what is possible with a photographic emulsion. The slightest vibration during the exposure—somebody walking down a neighboring corridor, a truck driving by—blurs them out. Even the light waves used to illuminate the scene to be recorded must all be of exactly the same frequency or wavelength, which means that holograms recorded on emulsions must be monochromatic.

In theory the use of emulsions could be sidestepped by using computers to calculate and print the image. Alas, there is a demon on that bridge, too. A 2-D representation reflects the same image, not counting perspective distortions, in all directions; it can achieve a reasonable level of graphics quality with a million dots (a dot being the smallest unit of visual information). A hologram has to reflect a different image in each of a large number of different directions; a million different directions would not be unreasonable. Building a pattern that could reflect a megadot pattern in each of a million different directions would require the computer to print out a trillion dots to equal the quality of a 2-D image. Further, hologram dots are more complicated than the dots in a 2-D image, so they take much longer to calculate and print.

These two factors multiply to a tremendous computational workload; the fastest contemporary supercomputers, which were barely imaginable in the 1960s, might require a hundred millennia working full-time just to generate a five minute, 16-image-per-second holographic animation. When the authorities responsible for allocating industrial R&D dollars understood that holographic snapshots of the Grand Canyon, let alone holographic TV, were *considerably* more than three fiscal quarters away, they dropped the technology down the hole. Today the Media Lab is one of the very few (perhaps the only) research lab still chasing the old dreams.

For many years now (Benton worked at Arc Mac on the same problem) the SIP team has been picking its way through the human spatial perception system, trying to find ways of evoking a convincing 3-D image with smaller and smaller amounts of information. We tend to move our heads from side to side, for instance, not up and down, so the holograms here do not work vertically: if you flex your knees or stand on tiptoe in front of the hologram gallery, the objects in the image do not slide over each other. Throwing that information away—telling the computers not to bother to calculate those dots—cut the calculation time by more than 99 percent. Since the distance between our left and right eyes, the targets of the process, tends to be fairly predictable, holograms don't need to reflect every bit of information in every direction, the way the real world does. Throwing away that information cut the calculation time by more than another 99 percent. Designing a hologram that is only visible to someone standing directly in front of the image saved even more time, etc. (On the other hand, reflections and highlights are critical to depth perception, so that information was kept.) So much information has now been discarded that the calculation time for each image is down to a few days, and the SIP team is still paring.

Eventually the team will get there, to the point where it will become practical to use a computer to generate 3-D images on paper, assuming the viewer examines them from exactly the right point in space, or even 3-D animations. It is an open question whether such a device will find a market. A hologram graphics printer would allow surgeons to interpret X-rays and CAT scans directly, without radiologists, and would certainly make a terrific presentation tool, but there are several other technologies that allow the perception of the third dimension; besides, there might not be any surgeons in 20 years. On the other hand, three or four generations from now the walls and ceilings of our homes might be covered with three-dimensional imagery.

The feeling on the rest of the campus toward Negroponte (at least in my experience) varies from indifference to bemusement, with isolated pockets of respect for his success at funding a research facility almost entirely from industry in an age when academic engineering is usually funded by the government. Most view the Lab as a lightweight, something of a theme park, not involved with problems worth a grown-up's attention. Certainly when one atmosphere is compared with the other, the rest of MIT seems tense, concentrated, grimy, a community of grunts taking out the glitches hole by hole, while the Media Lab seems frothy and effortless, as if it were gliding into the future like a hawk on a thermal. On the other hand, this might be part of the front, the style; perhaps the sense that the transition into Tomorrowland is frictionless, even fun, and therefore inevitable and automatic, is part of the demo concept. (For what it's worth, the members of the Lab publish as often as anyone in the professional literature.*)

A rarer view is that the Lab is less a vision of the future than of MIT itself in a world in which the government never got involved with financing engineering research. In that alternate universe all academic engineering institutions would be aligned with some mix or range of industrial or commercial sectors. Some would pitch to manufacturing, like MIT once did itself, others to marketing and strategic planning, like the Media Lab does now. If the Cold War had never happened and the government had kept its dollars out of academic engineering institutions, perhaps today most of the Institute would be giving its ideas the same high-gloss rollout, modeling them in easy-to-grasp, executive-summary formats, projecting the same happy effervescence.

One project under way in the Lab these days is the design of animation software that manipulates images as though they were subject to real-world physics. At an extreme (the programs are now nowhere near this good) a user watching an animated game of softball would be able to type "the batter hit the ball over the fence" and have the program recognize which images were being referred to, calculate the distance between the batter and the fence on the scale being modeled, figure out how much force would have to be imparted to the ball for it to cover that distance, move the batter through the body positions appropriate to generating that much force, define the sound that would be made by the bat

*Every month MIT publishes a list of all the articles and preprints published or written by persons with an MIT affiliation. The ratio of publications associated with the Media Lab to those of all publications approximates the number of full tenured professors at the Lab to the total number at MIT.

hitting the ball that hard, and then move the ball over the display in the correct Newtonian trajectory.

The demo of the current state of the project is a video display of multicolored geometric objects (cubes, pyramids, spheres, cones) scattered over a flat grid, like minimalist sculptures on a plaza. So far this "microworld" knows about geometry, light direction (instruct the program to move the light source in the animation and all the objects shade themselves accordingly), perspective, the physical impenetrability of material objects, opacity, gravity, inertia, and air resistance (a light object falls more slowly than an heavy one). It even contains a rendering of a cockroach that wanders randomly around the grid, avoiding all the objects and edges of the plane.

The thrust of the project is to pack more and more physical constants into the software: friction, viscosity, optics, the flow of heat, stress and strain, acoustics, solid-liquid-gas phase changes, and the like. The more physical properties these animation environments embrace the more aspects of the engineering enterprise can be moved into the computer. A program sensitive to geometry and the impenetrability of material objects would allow an engineer to experiment with different packing schemes and assembly arrangements without actually dealing with real objects; one that knew about electrical behavior would allow an electrical engineer to design a circuit on a computer and then simulate its behavior to see how it worked—again, without ever touching a real part. The idea behind the Media Lab microworld is to gather as many of these properties as possible into a single world to see (among other ambitions) how powerful "animation engineering" can become.

To a substantial majority of practicing engineers the idea that the profession might divorce itself from direct contact with real physical nature to live in the lotus land of video engineering, as if engineering were fundamentally nothing more than a computer game, is preposterous. They feel nature is much too quirky, complex, chaotic, and dense to be satisfactorily simulated for any but the most routine and narrowly defined purposes, like the packing of parts in a volume. Still, the microworld project does at least raise the prospect that one day some demo will fizz its way out of the Media Lab and swallow the Institute whole, embracing and incorporating all its processes.

At one point during my own microworld demo I was asked to slip on a glove lying near the terminal. When I had pulled it on, a wire-frame hand, like a five-legged spider hanging in space, appeared inside the display, hanging above the geometrical landscape, echoing "inside" the terminal every motion I made with the gloved hand. I moved my real hand down, squeezed my fingers together, and raised it. Inside the display the wire-frame hand dipped, casting as it descended a widening shadow on the plaza, picked up a cone, and lifted it. "Why is this better than simply working from a keyboard?" I asked a graduate student. "Because I'm *in there*," he said, pointing at the screen.

My guide shifted the point of view of the display to the back of the cockroach, so that I saw the plaza as if straddling the creature's back. From this perspective the cubes and cones nearest at hand were as large as houses. The cockroach swung around and stumped off, dodging its way through the solids. The geometrical countryside streamed by on both sides. At one point it pulled next to a blue cone, which on the scale of the display rose just over my head. I leaned over, picked it up, and with a single flip of my superwrist sent it soaring into dataspace. I expected it to slow, find a point of perihelion, and crash somewhere on the plain, but it just got smaller and smaller, tumbling end over end, until it blinked out entirely.

NINE

Nanotechnology

In 1959 physics Nobelist Richard Feynman pointed out that in theory acts of engineering could be conducted within extremely small volumes, orders of magnitude smaller than any contemplated at the time. Specifically, nothing in physics prohibited the design and assembly of parts as small as a few atoms, as opposed to the trillions or quadrillions that go into the smallest design elements in a watch. If engineering on such small scales could be achieved in practice, remarkable possibilities would appear. Given a "font" (or code) whose elements were composed of clusters of a few atoms, every book, magazine, pamphlet, and newspaper ever printed, complete with graphics, could be stored in a volume the size of a credit card. Materials made to atomically precise specifications—identical numbers of the same atoms in identical volumes—would run at their theoretical limits of hardness or lightness or strength, as if they had stepped out of the texts. (The methods of materials manufacture in use then and now usually leave materials riddled with microcracks and dislocations or impurities, all of which impose severe performance penalties.) Surgery could be performed by tiny robots, which could be introduced into the body noninvasively, motor off to the site specified by the surgeon, and conduct the operation from inside the body, either automatically or through remote links to the medical world "outside." (Feynman called this "swallowing the surgeon.")

Speaking practically, however, a less hospitable environment for engineering is hard to imagine. A convenient measure of length in this domain (the nanometer: a billionth of a meter) is to a yard as a yard is to a distance more than 70 times the diameter of the planet; a useful unit of time (the nanosecond) is to a second as a second is to 30 years. From the point of view of the nanoscale we humans move like geological processes; we have the metabolism of mountains and the delicacy of volcanoes or asteroid strikes. The difficulty of controlling acts of assembly, of slipping gear A onto axle B, seems insuperable when A and B are a thousand or ten thousand times smaller than the smallest object visible under a microscope and bounce about thousands of times faster than we can hope to react. Certainly in Eisenhower's America Feynman's speculations were obviously just so much science fiction, and in fact the physicist seldom repeated his argument (though he never lost his interest in microdesign).

Yet only 30 years later not one but several different pathways have been found down to the molecular realm, each developed by a different engineering science. Electrical engineers are shrinking circuit features down to 10

millionths of a meter and hoping for smaller; genetic engineers are learning to program bacteria and animal cells to
manufacture a steadily widening range of molecules; bio-
chemists are introducing ever more ambitious modifications
into natural proteins; materials scientists are assembling
composite materials out of novel crystals, molecular clusters, and sheets of monomolecular layers; applied physicists
have found ways to pick up and arrange individual atoms
into specific patterns; computer scientists are writing molecular modeling software that can calculate the behavior of
molecules directly, which facilitates the design, if not the
fabrication, end of the process; and synthetic chemists are
turning the skills learned synthesizing naturally occurring
compounds to the fabrication of molecules and complex
molecular aggregates unlike any found in nature.

The differences between engineering at the top and
bottom of the scale ladder can be illustrated by the compar-
ative importance of tying things down. Up here the forces
based on the interactions of masses—friction, gravity, and
inertia—give stability to the locations and orientations of the
items in our lives. Boxes and bricks and stacks of lumber stay
where they are put, crimes against property excepted. Down
there, none of these forces have any practical significance. A
mass that shrinks while keeping the same proportions loses
inertia and weight by the cube of the reduction; if we used a
magic ray to shrink our car by a factor of 10, the new model
would weigh not 10 but a 1,000 times less. Expressing the
difference in weight between a gear or beam built out of a
few hundred atoms and its proportional counterpart on the
conventional scale might require 25 zeros, and quite possibly far more. If buildings had as little mass per unit of height
we would be able to boost a 50-story skyscraper into the air
with a single breath, with the wave of a hand. The impact of
a beam of light would knock it tumbling. An observer

descending the ladder would find the air filling with objects, like the free-flying livestock and barns in the Kansas tornadoes depicted by Frank Baum. The farther down, the thicker the flotsam and jetsam would grow. On the bottom rung, at the molecular domain itself, the normal mode of existence of any object not securely fastened to a surface or sealed in a solid is to be continually beaten about by the random thermal fluctuations of the nanosphere like a leaf in a hurricane.

One of the few ways of acquiring some control over the position and orientation of these tiny parts is by fixing a molecule to a known site on a surface of known chemistry and geometry. More important, any sort of engineer has to see what he or she is doing, and at present our techniques for taking portraits of molecules are so slow and imprecise, and require so much tuning and resolving, that the objects of interest must remain in place for periods that on their scale are the equivalent of centuries. Tying them down, chemically bonding them to the photographer's backdrop, ensures that the subjects will sit through the entire exposure. One learns these skills in surface chemistry, that brand of the chemistry profession specializing in the molecular interactions of fluids and gases with solids. Studying these interactions as natural phenomena has made surface chemists into experts at wielding them as tools, and especially into masters at the art of pinning molecules to static positions on the surfaces of solids, like specimens in a collection book.

Recently an apprentice in this craft, an MIT graduate student named Tim Gardner, picked a photo album off his desk and began flipping through the pages. "There were railroad tracks running through the town where I grew up," he said (this was Lodi, Ohio), "and sometimes we would have a wreck." Pages flashed by, showing flat fields of lines running in parallel arrays or zig-zagging or meeting at precise right angles, like lines on drafting paper or plowed fields or urban grids glimpsed from the air. "The whole town would turn out to look." Gardner twisted the book around. Photo after photo appeared of what looked like railways that had been bombed out, blown away, ripped up. In reality these "rails" were barely the width of a bacterium—the pictures had been taken through an electron microscope, at a scale halfway to the molecular realm—but the only clue to that was the quality of the light illuminating the devastation: dim, absorbed, as if the photos had been taken underwater. "This is what happens when you get excited," Gardner said, scanning the wreckage, blue eyes glowing.

Gardner is a member of a team known within the Institute as the Wrighton Group (after the Group's principal researcher, provost Mark Wrighton), with a general interest in the electrical and electronic properties of molecules. It is a measure of how far we have come since Feynman's 1959 speech that the Group intends to explore this interest directly, by sticking voltmeter probes right into the front and back of any molecule that happens to be of interest, just as (essentially) an electrician might use a meter to look for open connections in a fuse box. Specifically, they hope to take a pair of wires, plug one end of the pair to a measuring instrument "up here," shrink the wires until they reach molecular dimensions themselves, and finally complete the circuit by using the magic of surface chemistry to tie a single, individual molecule across the gap between the two.

When this operation becomes routine, the science of surface chemistry will have a new instrument in its tool kit: a molecular voltmeter that will allow observers to follow the motions of electron clouds as they migrate over different molecular landscapes. The members of the Group expect the technique to have a host of engineering applications as well. If the electrical properties of the molecule tied across the microwires happen to include a sensitivity to some feature of its environment, then that circuit could also serve as a microenvironmental sensor. A minute change down there would ring an alarm or move a meter or flip a bit in a computer up here. Many such molecules are known, perhaps the most famous being chlorophyll, which reacts to the presence of light by emitting electrons. If a molecule of chlorophyll were fastened across these wires the circuit would act like a molecular photodetector, to be used, for example, in any application requiring the measurement of light intensities at high degrees of spatial resolution, such as optical computing or high-resolution spectroscopy. (The development of molecular photocells is in fact a focus for the Group, though for technical reasons they do not use chlorophyll.) A molecule that emitted an electron in the presence of a chemical residue associated with some disease could be tied to a pair of tiny wires and poked through the walls of individual cells, perhaps by Feynman's robot surgeon, without even injuring the membrane. "Virtually any chemical in the biological or chemical world can be detected with these systems," Wrighton says.

Since miniaturization usually lowers the cost of an item (when manufactured in bulk), the development of molecular sensors might make it financially practical to equip our machines with chemical senses—technology like that used today in drug and bomb detectors. In an era of cheap sensors our air, drinking water, and swimming beaches could be monitored continuously for many hundreds of pollutants and other substances of scientific interest. A door might unlock at the scent of its master; a garage smelling carbon monoxide in its interior would throw open the windows; and food processors could signal the chef to add a touch more chervil, not that any self-respecting chef would admit to using such a device.

The first rung of Gardner's daily commute down the ladder of scale can be seen with the unaided eye, so long as squinting is not counted as aid. It consists of eight (four circuits are laid at once) flat pink featureless ribbons arranged around three of the four edges of an onyx-colored silicon square about the size of a ladybug. Under a 30-power stereoscope these ribbons look like highly stylized lightning bolts, zig-zagging in from three consecutive edges to the fourth. With every zig they neck in, shrink narrower, eventually losing a total of some 500 factors of width, falling far beneath the limits of visibility. At the fourth edge each wire connects to a single gold electrode, two millionths (two microns) of a meter wide, and separated from its neighbors by slightly less distance.

Sometimes when Gardner is running an electrical test on these electrodes, the thought of what he is working with, the miraculously diminutive nature of these geometries, will distract him for a moment and a trickle too much current will leak into the circuit. Instantly, down at the other end of the scale ladder, one of the gold electrodes will overheat and explode off the board, soaring into the molecular abyss, perhaps slashing an ambient bacterium as it tumbles back down to disappear into the laboratory floor. All Gardner can do then is take his sample to the electron microscope and make it into data of another sort: an image of the devastation that can be imposed on the nanoscale just by thinking about it.

Two microns is still an enormous gap compared to most molecular objects, but to a mind trained on the conventional scale there seems no obvious reason why Gardner and his colleagues couldn't just bond a couple of molecular threads to either end of the molecule of interest and then tie those to the electrodes, like two wires twisted together and suspended from either side of the Grand Canyon. Such an idea would miss one of the key differences between molecular and conventional engineering, which is that molecular artifacts must be able to put themselves together spontaneously, like a djinn condensing out of smoke. The focus of the art is necessarily less the design of specific objects than of manufacturing environments that then fabricate the desired item autonomously. Some analysts, like K. Eric Drexler of Stanford, expect the long-run importance of molecular engineering to be found less in new applications or lower costs than in the economic and social consequences of self-assembling technologies. Drexler points out that self-assembly need not be restricted to the manufacture of small items: whales and redwoods and indeed entire rain forests self-assemble. Once the process is understood it should be possible to manufacture almost anything anywhere by dropping the proper molecular seeds into a supply of the right chemical elements. Sea water would serve for most items; high-end self-assemblers might work in the desert. Manufacturing might become as decentralized as vegetable gardening is today.

To put the prospect of growing your next car in your backyard in perspective, however, at the present moment not even the most skilled surface chemist can design an environment that will permit a molecular thread to bridge a two-micron gap. The thermal storm is too wild and chaotic; anything that long and thin would instantly wrap around everything else in the neighborhood, especially including itself. Calculations suggest that to have any chance of staying both unentangled and suspended in the transport medium, the circuit-completing molecule can't be much longer than five billionths of a meter, one four-hundredth the distance currently separating the electrodes. Since for the time being two microns is about as far down the ladder as the MIT Microfabrication Facility, where the chips are made, can go, somebody in this team has to find a way of narrowing the gap between the electrodes by 400 factors.

Gardner starts by placing the chip in a high-vacuum furnace (a desk-size complex bristling with stainless steel tubes), fastening it upside down and at a slight tilt inside a quart-sized chamber, and then firing an electron beam at a block of platinum lying under the chip. Far below any hope of visibility the beam smites the platinum atoms into such extremes of activity that they break away from their neighboring platinum atoms and rocket upward, eventually ploughing into the "windward" side of each gold electrode. Instantly (by the standards of our scale) the atoms pile up into a drift, which slopes down toward the lee of the next neighboring electrode nearest the source. If this operation is done right, the drift—the shadow—will peter out just a bit short of the upwind electrode, leaving a tiny crack of uncoated nonconducting chip substrate running between the edges of two platinum surfaces. The reader might imagine holding a bowl at right angles to a light source, so the interior, concave surface is completely illuminated, and then tipping it so that a tiny strip of shadow appears inside the bowl just under the lip nearest the source. The illuminated parts of the bowl represent the parts of the circuit coated by the spray of electrically conductive platinum atoms; the strip of shadow is the insulating silicon dioxide.

So far Gardner has been able to persuade the leeward skirt of platinum atoms to creep up to within 100 nanometers of its nearest neighbor, which closes the gap between the electrodes by 20 factors. Many viruses would not be able to wedge themselves into a gap this size. The natural growth of hair would cross that distance in ten seconds. But Gardner cannot afford to be impressed, thinking as he must of where the next 20 factors of shrinkage are going to come from. "How can you hope to wring that much improvement out of the technology?" he was asked. The question amuses him. "We're going to work ver-r-ry carefully," he says with a grin.

The electrodes are one half of the assembly; the other is the molecular sensor. Each sensor will be combined in turn from three functional parts: a part that recognizes and bonds to and only to the anode electrode, the electrochemically active part (which does the actual sensing), and a part that recognizes and bonds to and only to the cathode electrode. (The Group expects to simplify this differentiation by fabricating the cathode and anode of slightly different metals.) Eventually, when the gap between the electrodes has narrowed sufficiently, billions of these tripartite molecules will be synthesized and dissolved in a transport solution. The electrodes on a chip will be swept clean of garbage molecules (mostly hydrocarbons from automobiles, one of the few signs available on the nanosphere of urban life) with a beam of high-energy particles, and then lowered into the transport solution.

The last step in the assembly of the system, the connection of the molecules to the electrodes, will be conducted by the thermal storm itself, which shuffles molecules through billions of combinations of contacts every second. This explosive exploration of every corner of molecular solution space ensures that all the anode-loving and cathode-loving parts will find their surfaces of interest instantly. (At least in the molecular domain, the essential precursor for a high level of order is a high level of chaos.) In moments billions of sensors will string themselves across the gap, connecting in parallel like a self-sewing seam.

For this vision to be real it not only has to happen: it has to be observed, which cannot be assumed on this scale. The chemical nature of a material is usually ascertained by "tapping" it with a beam of energy, acquiring the echo resonating back and identifying it. (Every chemical species "rings" in its own characteristic way.) Such techniques were developed for conventionally scaled samples, with masses like those of grains of rice or peas or even marbles. From the point of view of the nanoscale these are continents; even the lowest power setting on the tools ordinarily used in such interrogations would rip into a monomolecular structure like a welding torch brought down on a bug. In the terms of the original analogy, molecular engineers are in the position of a bell-ringer playing his instruments with a 255mm howitzer.

Recently another member of the team, Jay Hickman, a strapping, exuberant guy with a sweeping mustache, took one of these instruments (a scanning spectroscope) apart and rebuilt it to express a beam of energy much weaker than the weakest available under the standard settings. The engineers working for the instrument company had good reasons, which they shared with Hickman, to suspect he was wasting his time: he'd weakened the interrogating beam almost to the background noise level. Even if his sample survived he'd be listening for a whisper in the middle of traffic. Hickman felt he had no choice: even at power levels just above background the instrument beam still cooked the sample. It was possible that at that level the sample would survive just long enough to radiate a coherent signal back up to the instrument; maybe not, too, but higher levels would have destroyed even that hope.

The spectroscope reported its findings graphically, and Hickman uses the analogy of searching through thousands of photographs of a forest trying to recognize one particular tree. (All the other trees being artifacts of the background.) "I spent months glued to the machine," he says. "Tweaking it a little bit, trying to see what had happened, to figure out if what I thought had happened really had happened, then tweaking it again. And with every observation I knew the sample had changed. Or been destroyed." Eventually he began to be able to pick his tree out from all the others, though even he cannot say quite how he learned to do this. When asked all he says is: "I just became one with the instrument."

One Spring day Gardner was reviewing some of the issues of self-assembling technology, what was and was not known about lifting parts into the field of diffusion. At one point a spontaneous thought interrupted him. "I wonder what the forces on a molecule falling out of solution are?" he asked. This was not a routine question, and he stopped to muse on it. Gravitational forces are not usually counted in molecular mechanics, but they must exist. Oil does float on water. Perhaps there are unusual, complex contexts in which gravitational forces might be important even in molecular interactions. The sun was pouring through the windows, and under its warming, wine-like influence, the conversation relaxed and opened out. "How many Gs does it pull?" Gardner turned to look out the window into the sky. His blonde hair ignited into a penumbral torch. "What does it feel like to be a molecule?" His voice was so low I could barely hear him. He squinted into the sun, while the fleet and subtle lives of molecules flowed through the room.

TEN

Technical Sports

The automatic maze solver mentioned briefly in chapter 6 had an unusual function for a piece of hardware: It was a philosophical argument, a comment on the controversy then lighting the skies over academia as to whether machines could learn, now or ever. As usual in such matters, the debate had become mired in disagreements over definitions. To some it seemed obvious that if you could change a machine's behavior by throwing a few switches, then the machine had "learned" the new switch configuration. To others it was equally patent that "true" learning, "real" learning, was something more than that; generalizing from the input in some nontrivial way, perhaps, or knowing what the data meant, or acquiring it autonomously, or applying it in some original manner, or even being conscious that learning was taking place.

Claude Shannon tried to cut through all this blather by pointing to the formal, scientific, objective definition of learning that had been coined by experimental psychologists: learning was what a maze runner displayed by avoiding alleys found to be blind on previous runs. (If this *wasn't* learning, then 40 years of research on the topic might as well be put to the torch.) He appealed to this argument in good engineering fashion not by writing an essay but by building an electromechanical lab rat (which actually looked more like a large mouse) that ran, solved, and remembered maze architectures as well or better than a natural rodent. The ''learning'' did not actually take place inside the mouse, but in a bank of relays built into a box under the maze. These drove levers that moved magnets over the underside of the maze surface, pulling the mouse through the gates and corridors.

When the mouse (which Shannon called Theseus) started a run the magnets tugged it in a straight line until its nose, which was loaded with contact sensors, detected the presence of a wall. These impacts would be communicated to the relays, which would instruct the magnets to pull the mouse back, turn it around, and poke its nose in a new direction. After some period of exploration Theseus would blunder into the goal and be replaced at the starting gate. During his second run the relay logic would subtract out the blind alleys the mouse had wandered down the first time. (If Theseus moved two steps to the right and then two steps back over the same squares in a subsequent run, that turn to the right would be evaluated as a blind alley.) This allowed the little vehicle to home in on the target without a wasted step.

The theory was that an observer watching the transition between the first, bumbling phase and the second, directed, run would feel foolish denying that the machine had learned. While the device failed to settle the arguments over the authenticity of computer learning, which proceed to this day, it did attract a fair amount of notice, both in and outside of the profession. *Life* magazine ran an article, titled, inevitably, "A Better Mouse." (The pictures of Shannon show a wolfish-looking fellow with a hatchet face, black bushy eyebrows, one of which is arched, and large, almost goblinlike ears. He is twisting his body to one side, leaning forward, looking up; a small mouth is pursed into an impish grin.) The legend of Theseus had so much persistence that almost 30 years later the organizers of a trade show decided to reenact it as a color event to spice up their conference.

Though I haven't been able to locate anyone present at the scene, it seems probable that the executives behind the 1979 National Computer Conference were interested less in probing the authenticity of machine learning than in demonstrating the promise and power of today's fine computer products in guiding our embattled business leaders through the complex decisions and stressful atmosphere of the corporate maze. Certainly several of the changes made in the Shannon protocol moved the contest in the direction of this narrative. For one, the micromice were to be entirely autonomous, carrying their own control, power, and energy sources (computers, motors, and batteries). This independence was to be expressed in a display not of learning but expeditious problem solving in a competitive environment: each mouse was to be set down in the maze and charged with arriving at the target faster than the competition.

Measured by how well it told this story, the contest was a disaster. Only one entry even reached the goal; the rest spun their wheels or ran into walls or got caught on gates. Even worse, the sole finisher had no computer; it just leaned against and raced along one wall (which braced it against the accidents suffered by the other entries) until it reached the goal, where it fell out of the maze to victory. Maze racing would have died on the spot had not some Britons visiting the conference seen that the wall-following strategy could be defeated by bringing the goal into the center of the maze and isolating it with free-standing walls.

When they returned home they held a European contest; this was seen in turn by some Japanese engineers who brought the idea to their country. Here maze racing went big time: clubs sprang up by the hundreds in high schools, colleges, and companies. An industrial robot company built a series of micromouse "police"—mice in police uniforms that tore up and down mazes with sirens and lights flashing—and sent them on a tour. A national competition was organized. Micromouse magazines appeared; kits were made and sold. A world championship tournament was announced, to be held in 1985.

While there might be a Japanese institution that does things by halves, the Japanese Micromouse Association is not it: the JMA defined a maze standard (a square 10 feet on a side divided into a grid of 16×16 squares, black floor, white walls), sent built copies free to any corner of the globe expressing interest, made tournament organizers available on request, and paid the travel expenses of the national winners. The contest was held in a converted theatre in Tsukuba, where interest was so intense that a huge TV screen was hung on the building so spectators could watch the action from the street. Judges from different countries were escorted to their seats by uniformed guards carrying their national flag while a band played that country's anthem. The emcees were professional TV personalities; politicians gave speeches and awarded the prizes; waves of enthusiasm rolled down all day long from those lucky enough to have seats. There were more than two hundred entries, most from

Japan, with the rest coming from elsewhere around the Pacific Rim. Of the 14 European entries, only one finished. (There were no American entries.) The excuse carried back to the other side of the hemisphere was that the European robots had been overwhelmed by their first experience with television lights.

A few weeks after the event the contest statistics were being passed around MIT, where they were examined with special attention in the corner responsible for developing the theory of electrical motors (superconducting motors, motors built with integrated circuit techniques, motor simulators, and so on). Apparently the times, including those of the winners, looked intriguingly high: If you looked at the geometry of the maze, figured out an average run, and then divided by the times posted, the numbers suggested that the Japanese were not using even the best motors available off the shelf, let alone the best that could be built. The numbers raised the prospect of an interesting bit of technical sport.

Technical sport differs from conventional sport in that the focus of the audience's attention, the entity out on the field, is a "team" of natural properties and processes. No matter how many dollars a conventional sport spends on engineering, it rests at bottom on the anthropocentric fantasy that a pure heart and a passion for the game can transcend the limits of physiology and even physics itself; that human desire can will nature into submission. The technical sportsperson is as enthusiastic about the transformative power of sports, but rides it in the opposite direction: the pleasure of seeing (what looks like) inorganic nature come alive in the quest for the perfect run, the personal best, the ultimate mesh.

Perhaps some day the Olympics will have a dozen technical sports, but for the moment MIT is one of the few corners of the culture where the concept does not seem alien. Technical sports represent both a refuge from the relentless piling up of logical abstractions and the chance to approach what might be the ultimate end-state of engineering: the self-using tool. The software libraries of the Institute are packed with predatory computer programs that hunt one another through the one-dimensional warrens of computer memory; at midsemester break robots play laser tag over the floor of the faculty dining room. MIT students enter most of the specialty contests, like building human-powered airplanes or submarines (granted, there are humans in these machines, but they are little more than power sources). There is even a course here, Mechanical Engineering 270, that teaches its subject (design) in the context of technical sport. No doubt MIT would have had an entry in the Tsukuba contest, but communication between the Institute and the JMA had somehow gone off track.

I n any event, the right people finally knew about the sport. Down in the basement, under the Great Dome, an instrumentation engineer named Dave Otten cut a small rubber disk off a test tube stopper, hooked it to a meter, and dragged a board across it. According to the meter, you could get a full G of traction out of this commonplace material before it broke from the board. At one G, after one second the mouse would be going about 20 miles an hour; after two, 60 miles an hour; after three . . . And Otten knew there were motors that could push even a moderately heavy mouse at one G. "We thought we could just muscle our way in," he told me. The world championship had restimulated some interest on this continent, and another competition had been announced for Atlantic City in March, 1986. Otten threw together a team of seven students, who combined the attention to detail and bold technical imagination for which MIT is famous by building an entry that came in last in a field of four.

When Otten is forced to speak of the Atlantic City episode, his eyes drop and wander over the floor; his voice grows faint; he laughs nervously. Though years distant, the memory still seems to make his skin crawl. "We missed a lot of things, I guess," he says. "Who were the other entries?" he is asked. "UCLA," he mutters. I wait. Several seconds creep by. "And Irvine." After this debacle (Irvine!), sheer nerd pride forced the team to get grim about maze racing. In July of that year his team showed up at a London competition. "That mouse didn't do anything clever," Otten says. "It just worked in its own simple way." A year after that Otten and Co. won the London event, becoming the maze-racing champs of the West. The Japanese did not appear at these events; their mice were so much faster that attendance would have been pointless at the least and perhaps even politically maladroit.

As Otten worked his way into the details of the sport, running mice over and over in different mazes, first in computer simulations and then physically, he found the trail of its essence leading in unexpected directions. Sports differ from ordinary human activities in that they depend on an unstable level of performance. You can no more make a sport out of what most participants can do most of the time than out of what no one can ever do. Maze solving is hard for humans given their weak grasp of distance and orientation (some amusement parks even have recreational mazes), but trivial for an entity that can keep an exact count of the number of steps that have been taken in which directions and the locations of every gate either passed or entered. (There is no very exact analogy to a maze for a computer anyway; to a machine, navigating the corridors of a maze is as procedurally cut-and-dried as following a straight line.) So there was little to be gained from polishing up the maze-solving algorithms; they were all about equally good.

Still less was maze racing a game of muscle. A maze racer runs in the face of a stream of events, unpredictable both in timing and degree, that are constantly pushing it off the correct course, parallel to the corridor walls. There are always minute irregularities on the maze surface, small bumps on the tires, and vibrations in the steering train, to mention only three. As these bumps and vibrations shove the machine off the parallel they naturally push it onto a collision course with one of the two walls. Contact with the walls or gates is always a risk, since destroying a wall could lead to disqualification and is usually fatal anyway, in that the bounces and skids and spins that follow leave the mouse disoriented and delayed.

The amount of time it takes a mouse to strike a wall, measured from the the instant some bump or irregularity first shoves it off its course, is a product of the amount of skew and the time required to cover the collision course. As the general speed of the mouse increases, the force of impact with any bump increases proportionately, which increases the angle of deviation, while the time to impact decreases. Thus the risk of wiping out goes up with the square of the speed. Even at moderate speeds, like two or three miles an hour, the little robots had enormous difficulty keeping a straight course down the middle of the corridors. What set their speed was not the power available, which was always more than ample, but the rate at which these deviations could be detected, measured, and corrected.

Computers existed that were fast enough on paper, but faster processors gobble electrons faster, which means they require larger and heavier batteries. Larger batteries make the mice either taller, imposing killing penalties on stability (forcing the mice to creep around corners to avoid turning over) or wider, requiring further debits from the corridor and gate clearance account, which was already overdrawn. Adding weight is usually going in the wrong direction, since the heavier the mouse the higher its center of gravity and the worse its stability (the fixed dimensions of the maze corridors made it impossible to spread the weight out horizontally). The one advantage of weight is that a heavy mouse going in a constant direction at a constant speed is less likely to be jarred from its course by a microbump. This is not significant, in that a properly designed mouse spends zero time in that state; it is always speeding up, slowing down, or turning. The Japanese had been using older motor technologies, just as Otten speculated, but not because they didn't know any better; even old motors had more than enough power to drive the mice into the walls.

In short, the sport as it was defined by the technology itself, by what the mice found hard, was about neither brains nor muscle but balance. From the mouse's point of view the task was to align halfway between two walls and then flow through an unpredictable set of course changes as rapidly as possible without losing grip of the middle way. The Japanese had seen this and designed the competition to showcase this feature, which was perhaps one reason why the sport had caught on in that country. They gave their mice an extended preliminary exploration phase, allowing them a practically unlimited amount of time to wander around randomly collecting information. Once a mouse had figured out the right path it was brought back to the starting line for the real contest: the speed runs. Each contestant had 10 attempts to get to the goal, with the fastest run counting as the official entry. Every time a machine spun out a team member could pick it up and fine-tune it for the conditions of the moment, changing the tires, cleaning the maze, or switching memories. In caricature the Japanese arrived at competitions not with completed entries but kits, building a new machine on the fly that was precisely tuned for each set of conditions.

The European race organizers developed a different set of rules that penalized both long search phases and tinkering during speed runs. The rationale advanced for these changes was to promote more intelligent and autonomous robots, which are worthy ends, though of course when losers pronounce the central strategy of their opponents illegal they leave themselves vulnerable to certain suspicions. Otten tried to build mice that could race under either regime. (Eventually the Japanese moved a step toward the European rules.)

When Otten returned from the London championship in 1987 he gave a public demonstration at Boston's Computer Museum on a full, standard maze, a matte black square of approximately one hundred square feet, divided by white walls about two inches high topped with red reflecting tape. By then he had built three mice; he brought two, each composed of a small metal oblong roughly the shape of a blackboard eraser and one or two rods held several inches out in front and off to one side, crosswise to the path of motion. The gestalt was that of the get of a roller skate and an electronic calculator, out dowsing for water.

The doll-like vehicles moved through the maze with two gaits: a slow, stately, and precisely rendered step-and-pause with the rhythm of a pavane; and dragster mode, racing for half the length of the corridor, coasting through the other half. During this latter phase the mice spun out again and again, impaling themselves on the maze posts or whacking into the walls. Twice the mice exploded in what looked like a tantrum of frustration: they would hang on a post and shove furiously in place, motor snarling, as if trying to rip the place

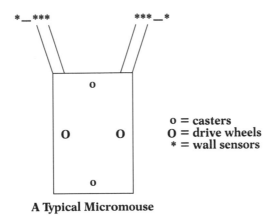

A Typical Micromouse

to pieces. "What causes *that*?" a member of the team was asked. His face sagged.

Throughout the demo visitors kept sidling up to Otten and asking, "So, what's the spin-off?" or "Why are you really doing this?" or "What's this good for?" Otten was then in his mid-30s, burly, with thinning blond hair, wide blue eyes, a snub nose, a round face, and a voice with an edge, the start of a rasp that 20 years from now will scrape bark off trees and paint from bricks. Whenever some variant on the practicality theme was put to him he would look away from the speaker, down at the floor or off at the action in the maze. He looked like an artist asked to explain what his work meant. "It's an instance of the general problem of independent motion," he muttered a couple of times. "They're, like, robots," a young man explained to his date. A couple of boys, maybe eight or nine, ran excitedly around the sides of the maze, keeping pace with the scurrying, buzzing machines.

Later Otten said he didn't say much about technical sports because experience had taught him that his audience wouldn't get it; they'd just keep repeating the same question or they'd be unbelieving or visibly appalled at the idea of an adult wasting serious skills and talents on such foolishness. If this is the sort of thing that goes on at MIT, was the attitude, no wonder the Japanese are kicking us all over the street. "When I was in London," Otten said later, "I did an interview for British television, and when I said I did this for the sport they understood. *They* got it. They didn't keep asking over and over. But the U.S. just doesn't seem to be into technical contests. Nobody wants to hear about this unless there's money involved. Look at the big solar car competition just held in Switzerland. Entries from all over the world, and only one from the U.S. And that was from MIT."

Like any other kind of engineering, maze racer design hangs between trade-offs: the mice should think as quickly as possible and they should think as comprehensively as possible, but they can't do both. They need to be light and they need lots of systems. They should be sophisticated and yet be dependable and buildable with a limited amount of time and money. Sooner or later every engineer speeding through this corridor in solution space hits a bump, gets a wrong idea, angles too far in one direction or the other, and wipes out. What restores this engineer often enough is the sight of a competitor's machine doing it right, breezing by that point in this metamaze as lightly as a ball balancing on the palm of a fountain. Working in a maze-racing backwater like the United States deprived Otten of this tonic and enormously lengthened the odds against his ever winning in the East. He gave talks, demonstrations, and lectures every chance he had at colleges and high-tech companies, the Computer Museum, and industrial conferences, but he was shouting into the void. Even Irvine and UCLA lost interest. During these months he sometimes sounded as if he was beginning to agree with the Computer Museum patrons: Why was he doing this?

In 1988 an invitation arrived from the organizers of the Ninth All-Japan Micromouse Final. Otten arrived with a brand new trick: running straight up "staircases"—connected series of 90-degree turns—instead of passively echoing the turns of the walls. The Japanese had not incorporated this ability into their own machines because they had anticipated that the local navigation problem would be too tricky: a mouse running down a corridor or making 90-degree turns can keep on course by holding a constant distance from each wall; for a mouse running up the diagonal the shortest distance to the nearest wall is constantly fluctuating. Otten resolved this problem by defining a higher order of features for the mouse to "read" —not absolute distance to a wall but distance from the *relationship* of the corner posts to one another. The MIT mouse came in third, winning the technical excellence award.

Otten made a videotape of the contest. Although he wasn't concentrating on the audience (he uses the tape to diagnose performance), you can hear a great whoop of excitement and delight rolling down from the stands when his mouse nosed into its first diagonal run. After the competition he and Kenji Mugita, chief engineer of the world champion team (sponsored by an industrial machinery manufacturer), took their machines and retired into a corner. Mugita does

Instead of this: **This:**

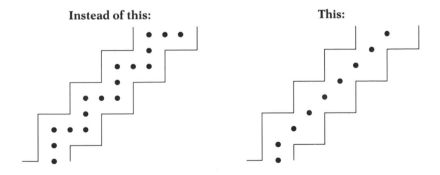

not speak English and Otten knows hardly a word of Japanese, but their expertise substituted for a common tongue. One party would finger a bearing and raise his eyebrows; the other, point to a hidden connector and smile. When Otten came back I asked him if he was still thinking of quitting. "Not when I've finally found someone to talk to," he boomed.

By his next trip, a year later, Otten was a full citizen of the maze-racing circuit. He arrived with something borrowed: the idea of measuring elapsed distance with a special wheel instead of counting the rotations of the main drive wheels. The special wheel ensured that distance would be recorded properly even if the drive wheels broke into a skid. (A design from Singapore had convinced Otten this was a practical idea.) He also arrived with a new contribution to the dialogue: pulling the wall sensors down inside the corridors, so the mouse looked like a little car, which improved both stability and clearance. Everybody was running staircases on the diagonal.

In 1991 Otten started winning contests in the Pacific Rim countries and for a few months was the undisputed world champion, an event that passed without notice in the American media (the MIT organ ran a few sentences). Since then he has bounced around in the top two or three places. The future of maze racing, the pursuit of finer and finer degrees of balance, stretches ahead: models with antiskid braking, suspension systems, four-wheel drive, and faster sensors are built or building or on the boards or on his mind. "Cutting metal," he says happily, when somebody asks how things are going.

In February 1992 an electric power society sponsored a contest in Boston and 15 entries showed up, most from this continent, by far the largest field to date in an American event. (About a third from MIT, only a subway ride away.) Most of the entries got jammed or stuck or racked up; watching the little robots struggle through the corridors made it obvious how difficult a sport this is. Three or four times one of the entries—one of Otten's mice, one of the Japanese entries, or a couple of extraordinary tricycle-like models built at the Ecole Polytechnique in Montreal—would build up a head of steam. Whenever this happened the audience made the same sound I had heard on the videotape of the Japanese contest: not a traditional sports cheer, since there was no one to cheer, but a wave of light-hearted excitement, amused pleasure, and a note of surprise. It was as if the audience was struck by its own responsiveness, taken off guard by the energy of the connection it felt to the little machines as they went whirling around corners, surging up the corridors, juggling between the walls, driving toward the inevitable wipeout.

ELEVEN

Vision Chip

For the first millionth of an inch after a drop of milk is released from a beaker or pitcher, it floats along, apparently oblivious to the pull of gravity, losing altitude at an average speed of about a yard an hour.* Thereafter, microsecond after microsecond, as if falling rewarded experience in the art, the bead drops faster and faster. During the first thousandth of an inch it falls at about 1.5 feet per minute; the

---

*These numbers are arrived at as follows: if $d = at^2/2$, then $t = \sqrt{2d/a}$. This last expression is used to replace t in $v = at$ to arrive at $v = a\sqrt{2d/a}$, which is expected to be the formula for the velocity of an object after it has been accelerating at rate a for a given distance. The results are halved to express velocities described as averages, or as being achieved "during" a time period. (These figures ignore frictional losses to the air, which are negligible. At these velocities a low-density, compliant, medium like air flows smoothly out of the way of forms as streamlined as these.)

first tenth, 75 feet per minute. By the time a drop of milk released the average distance above a glass of tea strikes the surface, it might well be travelling at two feet a second or more.

Such speeds drive the bead through the meniscus, the clingy surface layer on which striders tiptoe, like a nail punched through cardboard. The greater density of water makes it impossible for the molecules in the drop's path to flow out of the way smoothly, forcing the drop to jam its way through the medium, to bulldoze the water aside and fracture the flowlines. The energies lost in this effort trigger a cascade of chaotic interactions that spreads out into the glass at the speed of sound (in water). There they organize an invisible conical wake of vortices and vortex rings, oscillating eddies, and twisting streamlines; a peacock's tail of dynamical fireworks.

The reserves of momentum built up as the drop fell through air are quickly exhausted. After a long quarter-second an observer on the other side of the glass will see the rate of descent of the whitish spheroid slow and its form flatten. When its velocity drops below the speed of the wake, the turbulent microstructures catch up to their parent, circulate over it, and throw it open into a flowering of lacy plumes and spiraling veils.

At this point the milk is no longer an engine but a guide, spilling through a random selection of the dynamic processes spinning and wheeling all through the glass, illuminating them as it wanders. An observer might read this story as a gloss on craftsmanship, in which an entity first creates a dynamic structure and then steps into it, highlighting a representative cross-section for inspection, as if in search of applause or feedback or a quick sale. A psychologist might make an association between the impulses that generate thoughts in the mind and then infuse them with consciousness. Physicists could be struck, perhaps even feel subtly mocked, by the astronomical difficulty of finding a formula by which the forms of these efflorescing geometries might be predicted.

A minority might sense something intriguing, even anomalous, in the speed and ease with which a glass of tea can solve a problem (the kinetics of a drop moving through fluid) so hard that a mathematical physicist couldn't calculate with any precision even its difficulty, let alone find the answer. (At the very least, such a forecast would require measuring the velocities, vectors, and rotational moments of a quadrillion quadrillion molecules to subatomic levels of precision and then following each of these particles through a quadrillion interactions.) To a certain sort of mind, the ease and speed with which the glass of tea deals with the issues of its own becoming suggest not a different kind of mathematics but a different, and better, kind of mathematician.

In 1970 a graduate student in engineering at Princeton University named John Wyatt (MIT '68) found himself drawn into the orbit of these ideas. These processes are of course not unique to glasses of tea: The life of the world—the clouds overhead, a bit of froth dancing on a stream, a bar of music carried through the air, the ripples of muscles, and the electrical waves that dance through brains—all emerge from very large numbers of small objects communicating through waves of local interactions. These are the tools with which nature reasons, by which it composes and advances itself. Wyatt remembers being especially struck at how these processes draw no line between question and answer, between the presentation of the problem and its solution. The natural question transforms spontaneously into its own answer. "They don't wrestle with theory," says Wyatt, now a gentleman in his mid-40s with a warm, informal manner.

This seemed remarkable, enviable, and the student began to look for ways to cast these systems into research material. Ordinarily something is said to be "understood" when the various configurations of its elements can be mapped over time, permitting statements of the form "state A causes state B, which causes state C." While the huge numbers of calculations in natural systems put this kind of understanding out of reach, other kinds of descriptions, more statistical and atemporal, are possible—summaries not of the order in which the system ticked through its possibilities, but of how often it will reside in various configurations or relations, such as different orientations or speeds (or ratios of orientation to speed). Given two or three or four of these behaviors, the total package of possibilities along those dimensions could be constructed as a single image inside a two- or three- or four-dimensional graph. This form would be the solution space of every possible path of development open to the system; a top-down view of all the lives it could lead.

Wyatt specialized in defining these time-free, acausal, dynamic geometries as they appeared in electrical circuits. The context was simpler than most of the examples he saw in nature, more tractable, and yet it preserved one of the basic properties of natural processes: the simultaneous and cooperative interaction of all the elements. While the diaphanous, fantastical, and elegant shapes that emerged in these spaces were not the traditional results looked for by mathematical physicists, Wyatt's papers were well received, offering as they did an oblique look at an otherwise unapproachable phenomenon. In 1979 Wyatt was invited to join MIT's Electrical Engineering and Computer Science Department. Still, despite this professional success, he never quite lost a sense of how far his equations remained from the core of his interests: the ripple of muscles, the circulating, oscillating eddies in a stream, the waves of electrons carrying thoughts through the brain. At one point he compared his papers with a few twigs broken off the outermost branches of a huge tree; at another, with a locked window behind which he sat and watched the phenomenon, nose to pane.

In 1986 Wyatt's department sponsored a lecture by a visiting luminary from Cal Tech, Carver Mead. Although his name appears only rarely in the national media, Mead was (and is) an authentic eminence, a national treasure. Twenty years earlier he had opened the door to the dominant technology of this end of the century by discovering, contrary to the consensus of the day, that extremely small transistors worked as well as those that were merely small. Fifteen years after that, together with Lynn Conway, he simplified the logic of integrated circuit design so radically that tens of thousands of garden-variety systems designers were able to enter a medium that had been the exclusive playground of a few hundred supremely gifted craftspeople. These two peaks are only the most famous chapters of the career of a man naturally drawn to the biggest and most difficult problems on his intellectual horizon, and who somehow always found some way to scale them, at least partially.

By now Wyatt has forgotten many of the details of the lecture; what follows is drawn both from his recollections and Mead's published writings on the lecture topic. He certainly remembers the basic theme: Mead had taken another leap, this time into neurophysiology, into what Mead called the "operating systems of the brain," the deep structures that coordinate the interaction of the senses and acquired knowledge. A tremendous amount of work had been devoted to uncovering these (Mead said), but thus far to depressingly little effect. The reason was perfectly clear: science advances its understanding of large systems by studying smaller, simpler, examples of those systems, and in this case there are no such systems. Even insect brains are too interconnected, too intertwined, for their functions to be separated and studied in isolation. There were no "toy" systems left on which to test rival hypotheses of neural action. "Billions of years of evolution have presented us with highly efficient, highly integrated, and impossibly opaque systems," Mead has written and probably said.

Forty years ago a machine had been invented that some hoped might serve this purpose. Computers were far more brainlike than any other machine then in use: they used electricity to process and store information, translated data into different levels of symbols or representations, and were composed of many small elements that were constantly switching on and off, like neurons. Though not biological in every respect—they were dry instead of wet, to mention only the most obvious point—there were enough points of similarity to imagine that the machine could serve as the primitive, ancestral, brain long since discarded by evolution.

Enough time had passed to take stock of these expectations, Mead suggested, and conclude that the computer-as-brain model had made only the most minimal contribution to neurophysiology. The reason was not (as some philosophers thought) that the brain was inimitable, but that the analogy had not been pushed far enough: digital computers were not *enough* like brains to serve the purpose. It was possible to build a computer that embodied the principles of neurophysiological operation to a much more intimate level of detail. In fact, Mead was organizing a project at Cal Tech to take this very step: to construct the nearest thing to a real brain possible with contemporary technology. If the project succeeded, neurophysiology would have two legs to advance on: research into structure, to be conducted with microscopes pointed at neural tissue, and research into function, as expressed in a series of progressively more complicated silicon brains.

He planned to start with the retina, a tiny speck of neural tissue loosely attached to the inside rear surface of the eyeball. No part of the brain was better understood: Its input (the image projected on its surface by the lens) could be defined exactly, and the location of its output was known to a certainty (the optic nerve) and could be monitored with confidence. Its general functions—converting pulses of photons into pulses of electrons and then compressing the output of its hundreds of millions of rods and cones (the biological photometers) so they could be carried back into the skull by the optic nerve—were well known. A person building an artificial retina could be confident of measuring just how close that device had come to the real thing. No other part of the brain met this standard. Finally, the essentially two-dimensional structure of the organ made it easier to "copy" into silicon using the integrated circuit fabrication techniques of which Mead was so consummate a master.

An example of how Mead planned to make his artificial retina more biological, more brainlike, is his solution to the problem of distinguishing changes in illumination (as when the sun moves across the sky) from physical changes in the scene, like an animal moving over a field. In general, seeing entities, be they natural or artificial, are far more interested in learning about physical changes than shifts in background illumination, yet both causes are mixed together in the shifting patterns of intensity changes that fall on the retina. Both evolution and machine vision engineers have had to find ways to prevent changes in background illumination from interfering with the analysis and recognition of the movement going on in a landscape. Both began with the observation that changes in illumination tended to be comparatively diffuse, general, and pervasive, which meant that an average intensity value, calculated over many photosensor readings, was a good measure of background illumination.

Past that point evolution and engineers worked different sides of the road. Machine vision engineers used the tools of digital computation (memory, a processor, a program) to attack the problem as follows: first, a grid of photosensitive elements would be exposed to a scene. The program would then instruct the processor to read each element one at a time, translate its intensity measurement into a number, and store that number together with the address of the originating element in memory. When all the elements had been surveyed, a routine would use these values to calculate one of the many possible different averaging formulas (averages can be calculated over space or time or a combination of dimensions). This average is stored in memory. Next, a second routine summons the original values back out of memory, subtracting this average from each one. (In theory this operation should highlight only the intensity variations caused by physical changes.) Finally, the corrected numbers are copied back into memory and passed on for further processing. In theory (the problem is not yet completely solved) this sequence of operations should make it possible for a machine to see the same objects in the same way regardless of changes in the brightness or direction of the illumination of a scene.

The biological retina uses a completely different strategy; what Mead called "the strategy of collective systems." An analogy might be to a huge field of buckets—square miles of them—over which a few rain clouds are passing. If these buckets are not interconnected, they will fill up and lose their ability to register changes of kind. If they are interconnected correctly (no small qualification, that) with little tubes, the net as a whole will "adapt" to the rain storm. In that condition the grid will be able to register the spray from a garden hose even in the middle of a shower. The slow changes characteristic of environmental illumination cannot

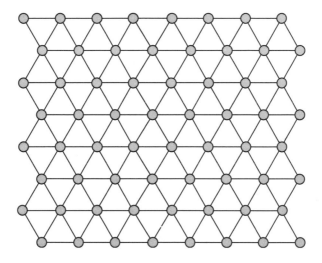

accumulate and therefore cannot be detected; fast changes overwhelm the exchange capacity of the network, do accumulate, and can register. Mead planned to build a retina around the field of buckets plan, around a system of interconnected neighbors, only out of silicon instead of carbon.

Because Mead was speaking at MIT, as opposed to Harvard Medical School, it is likely his proposed chip was appraised from an engineering perspective. One aspect of his design that must have drawn the attention of the audience immediately was that it was not programmable; there was no array of memory elements in that "field of buckets" in which instructions could be stored and no central processor to execute them. This might have made a world of sense from a neurophysiological point of view, but to an engineer it was a repudiation of one of the major achievements and continuing trends of contemporary engineering: getting design logic out of physical parts, physical structure, and into software or programming.

If the averaging and recalibrating functions described above were performed by software, for instance, a person wishing to tinker with them would need to do nothing more than sit down at a keyboard and rap out the code. Mead's chips were fixed, inflexible; each cycle of generate-and-test would require the construction of a physically new specimen. From this perspective, as Wyatt suggested, his lecture might as well have been on steam-driven automobiles. No doubt a smart mechanical engineer could find much of interest to say on the subject, but the topic was not likely to go anywhere. General Motors, for instance, was unlikely to be interested.

Paradoxically, it was this very lack of programmability that brought Wyatt down out of the audience, stammering with excitement. To the engineer the absence of a computer spelled a machine that "didn't wrestle with theory," a machine in which problems transformed into solutions, in which answers were generated directly by locally interacting neighbors communicating in waves. In a programmable, digital, retina the rhythms of nature were made to sit and wait at the chip surface while a processor transcribed the photon intensities into symbols, ran a complicated program on those symbols, and transcribed the product of the routine back into signals to pass up the circuit for further processing. In Mead's chip the inputs and outputs were dynamically, physically related: waves of photons landing on the surface of the chip pushed waves of electrons out through the underlying circuitry. Nature could reach right into the machine and create the desired result all by itself. "I was stunned," Wyatt says. "He'd gone and done it. He'd done a little bit of the right thing." The mathematician remembers crowding up to Mead after the lecture, telling him over and over, "This is so gorgeous."

As he walked out of the lecture hall Wyatt found himself hankering after a bit of the right thing for himself. "I was wondering how I could bring some of this excitement to

MIT," he says in a warm, tenor voice. "MIT is kind of a . . . " here Wyatt paused for a beat ". . . stringent place." Merely doing "the right thing" was not enough.

By one reading of the cards his chances were not good: Wyatt was a theoretician, with no expertise in machine vision or the managment of engineering research projects, and the collective systems approach to chip design was no small tweak. It proposed taking information processing technology back to a new starting line, a new year 1, as if the decades of development conducted under the auspices of the programmability paradigm had never occurred. Every aspect of the traditional approach to machine vision would have to be rethought and rethought synchronously: the hardware redesigned to support whatever the new processing strategies would be (the "field of buckets" being one example), and the traditional processing strategies of machine vision redesigned to fit the hardware.

On the other hand, although the programmability paradigm was still going from triumph to triumph in the culture at large, there was a category of issues against which it had been beating its fists for years with no results: those having to do with plugging computers directly into the natural world, as opposed to feeding them preprocessed data or placing them in environments designed from the start to support computer activity. This limitation had been apparent from the earliest years of the technology. In the 1950s and 1960s a journalist looking in at Carnegie-Mellon, MIT, or Stanford could see that computers' abilities were never very general: the images they recognized had to lie quietly against a specified background under a known, constant, illumination; speech recognizers could deal only with the voice of a given speaker with a small, specified, vocabulary; robot hands could pick up only objects with a very tightly defined set of geometries.

Almost everyone attributed these limitations to the youth of the technology; the first airplane, the first automobile, the first television—each had had a pretty restricted range of function as well. There seemed to be no reason to assume that the computer engineers would not be as successful in scaling up the range of function for these devices. Certainly the engineers had no inkling of any special difficulty in coupling the machines to the real world.

Given this level of optimism, it seemed reasonable, even prudent, to expect some extraordinary changes. Several conferences were held in these decades to prepare for the end of labor, when the curse lain on Adam and Eve would be lifted, perhaps to be replaced by the greater curse of chronic idleness and dependency on technology. But the expectation of scalability was unfounded; computers turned out to be nothing like jet engines or automobiles. Over and over again the machines proved unable to survive the smallest step out of the laboratory toward real-world conditions. A machine that could pick up clean blocks failed totally when the blocks were dirty, or came in a variety of sizes, or had to be recognized under a range of lighting conditions, or were presented in a jumbled pile. If somebody tried to write a program to deal with dirty surfaces, it always seemed to turn out that there were 60 different kinds of dirt—granular dirt, greasy dirt, sticky dirt, dirt that changed the outlines of the block— each requiring unique treatment. Some researchers hoped that "low-level" faculties such as vision and hearing might generalize more easily than "higher" cognitive powers such as description and explanation, but painful experience showed that any skill or task, higher or lower, that required cutting through the noise and flux of the real world and grasping its underlying continuities got stuck in the same bog.

Fortunately for the industry, simultaneously with this failure engineers working on other questions found a large number of useful things computers could do with formalized, processed, purified data: spreadsheets, databases, digital communications, and the like. The industry that grew up around manipulating these libraries of sanitized information was so successful that the earlier expectations were almost forgotten; few expect to see machines walking city streets, driving cars, or carrying on conversations in their lifetime, and no one ever talks about the end of labor any more.

When Marvin Minsky, founder of the MIT Artificial Intelligence Lab retired, he summed up his experience as testifying that minds are not the single, connected, coherent entities envisioned by terms like *consciousness*, but inter-communicating aggregations of hundreds or even thousands of different microintelligences, each with a unique set of methods, memories, and purposes. To read depth properly, for instance, the mind must have one organ capable of comparing two images of the same scene taken from slightly different angles or times, another weighing changes in shading, a third that measures the degree of focus necessary to resolve a scene, a fourth that retrieves prior knowledge about the scale of objects, a fifth that filters out information on overlapping, a sixth that measures the proximity of objects (the farther away two objects are, the closer to each other they appear), and a seventh that is sensitive to changes in resolution (the more distant an object, the less detail is visible).

Each looks out at the world in its own way, searches for a different set of features, works more or less dependably according to the external situation, and has its own ideas about how to structure memories and format sensor reports. They run simultaneously, artisan-technicians in a society of minds, an ecology of intelligences, feeding their conclusions back and forth as if in a miniconference about the scene immediately at hand. In the end they resolve their disagreements as best they can in the time available, occasionally making a very poor call.

What is true of depth perception seems to be true (Minsky thinks) not only of other aspects of vision, like the perception of color and motion, but of most other categories of cognition, from motor control to the development of the most sophisticated metaphors and connections to the methodologies that coordinate and resolve the interplay of these microintelligences. The theory dramatically contradicts our introspective feelings of how we occupy our own minds, but it at least provides a simple explanation for why building a machine competent to deal with the natural world should take a long time.

Unfortunately, it also seems to predict that the very effort to design all these senses (and their coordinating functions) will end up digging the enterprise all the deeper into another mudhole. Many of these senses require large amounts of data to give reasonable levels of precision—a million measurements is not unusual (the human retina has a hundred million rods and cones). A sophisticated program of this sort might execute at least a thousand instructions in order to evaluate each data point, which multiplies out to a billion operations. Suppose further that the sense in question is intended to monitor a dynamic process, requiring many sensor readings to be taken every second. If the results are going to be delivered in real time, as fast as they come in, which would be essential for most robotic operations, this would set the work load of the processor at 10 or 20 billion operations a second *for a single sense.* Many industrial processes and consumer applications would require even faster measurement rates, particularly if the vision system was expected to be in motion itself, as might well be the case with robots.

If the application required dozens of senses, as research suggests it might, the total load would overwhelm any computer this civilization is likely to build for decades. (There has been speculation that the philosophers who argued that artificial intelligence was impossible were right for the wrong reasons: not because it is impossible to encode human intelligence in symbolic form, which is what the philosophers thought, but because once that had been done the program would take a hundred years to say hello.) In theory, this computational explosion might be contained by scaling down the functionality of the programs while continuing to make faster and faster computers, but now comes the third problem: the faster a computer is, ceteris paribus, the more power it takes. A computer fast enough to run a useful vision system, even assuming one could be built, might require tens of kilowatts. Such extreme power requirements, with all their depressing implications for cost and portability, radically limit the range of potential applications.

When a person with direct responsibility for approving grant proposals on this question—for pushing the programmability paradigm into natural, untreated, contexts—comes to work in the morning, these are the problems that are waiting: managing complexity; the implications of large power demands; and, most often, the endless, insatiable, relentless demands for more processor speed. Noon comes and this person takes sandwiches to a nearby park. A flock of pigeons wheels around the side of a building and lands nearby. In the trees overhead squirrels leap from branch to branch. Perhaps a flycatcher snatches mosquitoes out of the air, or mice scurry out from the grass to seize a crumb of bread. Across the street, in the park, a dog leaps six feet off the ground to intercept a Frisbee. Hummingbirds and honeybees swerve and loop through complex botanical sculptures. This soul is everywhere surrounded by scraps of neural tissue the size of a peanut, of a grain of rice, that run off the power obtained by digesting a few bugs or seeds, with operating cycles that run a million times slower than contemporary processors, executing feats of information processing that a ton of computers could not approach.

Wyatt's proposal was modest and focused and stringent, but these are formal virtues to be expected in documents of this class. There is always a role for the incidental in such decisions, for the influences of the moment. Perhaps he got his money because the program officers at the National Science Foundation and the Department of Defense had just come in from lunch in a park. In any event, by 1988 Wyatt had his piece of the right thing.

The short list of the meanings the members of the MIT Vision Chip Project hope their devices will extract from the world include sensing the speed and direction of camera or sensor motion from visual cues; recognizing the lines in a scene (i.e., the edges created by changes in shading, texture, and physical shape); and defining the distance of the various points from the lens. None would be considered a breakthrough: no item on this short list is unachievable by digital machines, and in aggregate they fall far short of defining a complete vision system, which would be able not only to distinguish physical objects from one another but to identify them (i.e., correctly associate them with whatever physical properties are relevant to the task at hand). Nor does Wyatt intend to duplicate the operating systems of the brain. A sensible person does not run against Carver Mead on his own track. The primary rationale of the Project is not to drag specific functions into practice (though that was certainly a secondary goal) but to make the case that the design intelligence now being imagined by programmers, packed into memory, copied into processors, and run on digitized data was out there already, ready to be filtered out of the natural world.

One of the first chips the Project built was designed to recognize the location and orientation of the brightest object in an image. Put together by graduate student David Standley, it works as follows: When a wave of photons strikes a region somewhere on the face of the chip, photoelectric sensors convert the wave into a pulse of electrons, which flows into a conductive network running off toward the edges of the chip. The network mixes it with charges from neighboring elements, automatically generating a limited form of correction for background illumination and random noise. When this mixed wave arrives at the edge of the chip it passes over some section of a string of electrical measuring devices set around the perimeter. An everyday analogy might be placing cups around the edges of a tray of water, dropping a rock into the tray, and weighing how much water slops into which cup; the cups nearest the point of impact will have the most water in them. In this case the location of the brightest area is the intersection of the sections of the perimeter registering the most charge.

Any digital computer can perform the same functions, because any digital computer can do anything any other computer, including any collective systems computer, can do. All that is necessary is to feed the machine the right list of instructions, which in this case might look something like this:

- focus an image on a grid of photosensitive elements;
- translate the intensity measurement made by each element into a number;
- store that number together with the location of the originating element in memory;

- filter out random noise and changes in background illumination (as described earlier);

- retrieve the adjusted values from memory and rank in order of intensity;

- throw away the less intense values;

- retrieve the locations in the image of each of the brighter values; and, finally,

- run a statistics program on these addresses to find the shape of the neighborhood defined by the largest number of brighter points.

Standley had replaced the instructions on this list with the properties of time, geometry, electricity, and silicon. The cost of this substitution was measured in the loss of universality: His chip could find the center and long dimension (which direction it is pointing in) of the region defined by the brightest points in an image and nothing else. If Standley wanted to run any other type of program, a computer game or spellchecker, he would have to find other facilities. But freeing his chip from the need to copy instructions and data in and out of memory at every point allowed it to cook along at an incredible pace for artificial sensory processing, reporting 5000 images a second, while drawing almost no power beyond the power of the signal itself.

Whenever Wyatt gives presentations on the Project at seminars, industrial workshops, and conferences, he usually finds a moment to step back and push the philosophy. "Dave's chip is evidence that by thinking about the material you can get 5000 frames a second," he might say, or "What we do is find out what silicon wants to do and get out of its way." An engineer of another age would recognize instantly that Wyatt was talking about a sense for the fitness of things. (In fact, on a systems level, in terms of basic architecture,

Standley's design is not so different from the networks of sluices, channels, gates, and metering wheels that MIT graduates were designing for the hydropower industry more than a hundred years ago.) That an MIT professor can be standing up and selling sensitivity to the properties of the natural world as a breakthrough concept in engineering speaks volumes on how the metaphysics of the profession has changed (in certain neighborhoods).

One reason the programmability paradigm so ignited the imagination was its compatibility with our model of the relation of minds to nature—that of two phases of existence so different it seemed a mystery that they could have any kind of relation at all. Nature is out there and minds are in here; nature is passive, open to any and every random influence, while minds have purposes and intentions; nature is blind and minds think; nature is determined and minds have choice; nature is a scattered flux of interacting particles while minds are coherent and unified. The model assumes that perception is our problem and that the only way to solve it is to figure the whole story out all by ourselves, down to the last element, and then rebuild every single brick in the process. It assumes that the brain brings perception to nature; that nature does not want to be seen.

The computer, with its single processor, enormous flexibility, and symbolic, thoughtlike, languages came as close as any physical machine ever will to looking like the mind side of this model. The tremendous effort to make the computer into a real mind followed naturally. The failure of that effort, or at least the tremendous resistance it has met, should throw the model into question. Perhaps in fact nature is full of short cuts to its own perception, short cuts that natural selection has found and gathered together into our own visual system. There are marine invertebrates which, when they swim, generate dynamical patterns in the water that echo and depict their proportions and body outlines. With every motion these creatures leave meanings cycling in their wake, fully formed, ready to be harvested. Each instrument in an orchestra trails its own pattern of sympathetic vibrations across the strings of the harp, describing its intensities, its life. Perhaps objects call their own perceptions into being in the same way, by evoking resonances in the brain. Perhaps perception is direct as that, a matter of like summoning like.

Of course there is no reason to draw the limits of the model around perception alone. Perhaps the effort to build machines that can operate freely in the real world—machines that can not only perceive but recognize and describe and understand—will teach us that handholds are everywhere out there, leading hints and flashing arrows and fingers with signs hanging off them that say "right this way," and "no waiting." If engineering is the art of finding the parts of nature that have the same interests you do and gathering them into a single form, then the metaphysics of this practice is that the kind of universe we live in is composed at least in part, and perhaps entirely, of elements whose behaviors matter to us, intimately. These resonances rise from every side; perhaps they are gathering us. It is impossible to decide whether humankind or nature is imposing its identity on the other, who is calling whom, where the field of attraction originates, whether each new idea brings you deeper into the world or deeper into your brain. It feels like both at once, and there is no obvious reason to impeach that testimony. What is clear from the long perspective of the Infinite Corridor is that we are mixing into a harlequin intimacy.

SELECTED BIBLIOGRAPHY

Bolt, Richard A. *The Human Interface: Where People and Computers Meet.* Wadsworth, 1984.

Brand, Stewart. *The Media Lab: Inventing the Future at MIT.* Viking, 1987.

Calvert, Monte A. *The Mechanical Engineer in America, 1830–1910: Professional Cultures in Conflict.* Johns Hopkins Press, 1967.

Dorsey, Gary. *The Fullness of Wings: The Making of a New Daedalus.* Viking Penguin, 1990.

Drexler, K. Eric. *Engines of Creation: The Coming Era of Nanotechnology.* Anchor Doubleday, 1986.

Geiger, Roger. *To Advance Knowledge: The Growth of American Research Universities 1900–1940*. Oxford University Press, 1986.

Hodges, Andrew. *Alan Turing: The Enigma*. Simon & Schuster, 1983.

Hunter, Louis C. *A History of Industrial Power in the United States, 1780–1930*. Vol 1., *Waterpower in the Century of the Steam Engine*. Eleutherian Mills-Hagley Foundation, University Press of Virginia, 1979.

Klemm, Frederick. *A History of Western Technology*. MIT Press, 1964.

Levy, Steven. *Hackers*. Anchor Press, 1984.

Mahowald, Misha A., and Mead, Carver. "The Silicon Retina" in *Scientific American*, May 1991.

Manning, Kenneth R., ed. *MIT: Shaping the Future*. MIT Press, 1991.

Marx, Leo. *The Machine in the Garden: Technology and the Pastoral Idea in America*. Oxford University Press, 1964.

Minsky, Marvin. *The Society of Mind*. Simon & Schuster, 1985.

Morison, Elting. *From Know-How to Nowhere: The Development of American Technology*. Basic Books, 1974.

———. *Men, Machines, and Modern Times*. MIT Press, 1966.

Noble, David F. *Forces of Production*. Oxford University Press, 1986.

———. *America by Design: Science, Technology, and the Rise of Corporate Capitalism*. Oxford University Press, 1977.

Pacey, Arnold. *The Maze of Ingenuity: Ideas and Idealism in the Development of Technology*. MIT Press, 1974.

Persig, Robert. *Zen and the Art of Motorcycle Maintenance.* Bantam Books, 1974.

Petroski, Henry. *To Engineer is Human: The Role of Failure in Successful Design.* St. Martin's Press, 1985.

Reintjes, Francis J. *Numerical Control: Making a New Technology.* Oxford University Press, 1991.

Sellers, George Escol. *Early Engineering Reminiscences (1815–40) of George Escol Sellers.* Edited by Eugene S. Ferguson. U.S. National Museum Bulletin, No. 238. Smithsonian Institution, 1965.

Sinclair, Bruce. "Inventing a Genteel Tradition: MIT Crosses the River." In *New Perspectives on Technology and American Culture,* edited by Bruce Sinclair. American Philosophical Society Library, 1986.

Turing, Alan M. "Computing Machinery and Intelligence." In *Minds and Machines,* edited by Alan Ross Anderson. Contemporary Perspectives in Philosophy Series. Prentice-Hall, 1964.

Turkle, Sherry. *The Second Self: Computers and the Human Spirit.* Simon & Schuster, 1984.

Weizenbaum, Joseph. *Computer Power and Human Reason: From Judgment to Calculation.* W. H. Freeman, 1976.

White, Pepper. *The Idea Factory.* Dutton, 1991.

Wildes, Karl L., and Nilo Lindgren. *A Century of Electrical Engineering and Computer Science at MIT, 1882–1982.* MIT Press, 1985.

Winner, Langdon. *Autonomous Technology: Technics-out-of-control as a Theme in Political Thought.* MIT Press, 1977.

Software (trade show catalog). *Information Technology: its new meaning for art.* The Jewish Museum, 1970.

INDEX

Abstract engineering, 50
Academic research
    environments, 78
Adams, Henry, 43–44
Aircraft, human-powered, 8–9
Animation software, 142–143
Apprenticeship system, demise
    of, 42
Architects and architecture,
    47–62
  disdain for, 53–55
  exploitation by, 129–130
Architecture machine,
    130–136
Architecture Machine Group
    (Arc Mac), 132–136
Arm, prostheses for, 115–117

Arnold, John, 110–111
Art vs. science, 59
Artifacts
  disdain for, 49
  natural behavior of, 79
Artificial intelligence, 74–75,
    187
Artificial Intelligence Lab, 105
Artificial knees, 118–127
Artificial retina, 179–192
Aspen Movie Map, 134–135
Atomic structure and
    nanotechnology, 145–156
Automated navigator, 138

Back Seat Driver navigator,
    138

Bacon, Francis
  on knowledge and power,
    50n
  on truth, 28n
Balance in maze racing, 165
Baldessari, John, 131
Basketball for blind, 114
Beauty contests, reverse, 84–85
Beck, Don, 23
Behavior
  of artifacts, 79
  psychology of vs. parts of,
    16–17
Benton, Steve, 139, 140
"Better Mouse, A," 159
Blanco, Ernesto, 1–7
Boston Arm, 117
Bosworth, Welles, 56–57
Brain, operating system of,
    177–178
Browne, Thomas, 51
Bush, Vannevar, 78

Cambridge, MIT move to,
    47–57
Canals, 29–30
Cash register, reprogramming,
    11–12
Chomsky, Noam, 89
Circuits, shrinking, 146–147
Cocooning, 135
Collective systems, strategy of,
    180–182
Colt, Sam, 27
Communism, threat of, 79
Competitiveness, 80–81
Compton, Karl, 66
Computers
  as brains, 178

invention of, 70–75
and nerds, 86
power for, 187
projected market for, 103
for prostheses, 116–117
and Tech Model Railroad
    Club, 102–107
for 3-D images, 139–141
Concept nerds, 85
Conway, Lynn, 177
Cost of excellence, 19
Craft nerds, 85
Croton reservoir, 29
Culture of connections, 18

Dataland, 133–134
Dennis, Jack, 105
Depth perception, 185–186
Design-through-debugging, 9
Desktop secretary, 137
Details and manipulations,
    knowledge of, 36
Displays, 15–16
Diversity-in-uniformity, 15–16
Drafting, 109–111
Drexler, K. Eric, 152
DuBridge, Lee, 66
Dupress, John Kenneth,
    112–113
Dust in model train layouts, 94
Dynamic processes, machine
    vision for, 186
Dynamo Lab, 64–65, 75

Eastman, George, 47–48
Educational reform, 34
Educational societies, 31
Elbow, prostheses for,
    115–117

Electromagnetic radiation, 67–68

Electromechanical lab rat, 98, 158

Employment of early graduates, 40–42

Engineering
frustration in, 5–7
productivity of, 87–88
whole vs. parts in, 17

Engineering sciences, 75–88

Engineers
as incrementalists, 64
as nerds, 82–86
in nineteenth century, 28–31
origin of, 26–28
vs. physicists, in radar development, 66–70
requirements for, 31
vs. scientists, 50

Execution nerds, 85

Expenses, increases in, 80–81

Eye, modeling of, 179–192

Fashion paradox, 2

Feynman, Richard, 65–66, 145–146

Fitness of things, 28–29

Flowers, Woodie, 120–126

Franklin, Benjamin, 37

Freeman, John Ripley, 51–57

Gait dynamics for artificial knees, 119–123

Galileo, 77

Games
maze racing, 157–171
Star Wars, 105

Gardner, Tim, 148–156

Generate-and-test cycle, 9, 69

Gifford, Frank, 106

Gödel, Kurt, 72

Goldfarb, Mike, 123–127

Gossamer Albatross, 9

Group study, 31

Guided iteration cycle, 9

Hackers (Levy), 105–106

Hacks, 92

Handicapped, prostheses for, 112–127

Hardy, G. H., 72

Harvard
disdain for, 57–58
and MIT move to Cambridge, 48–49

Hickman, Jay, 155–156

Hodges, Andrew, 73

Holography, 138–144

Human interfaces, 135–136

Human-powered aircraft, 8–9

Hunter, Louis, 30

Hydropower, 30–31

Incrementalists, engineers as, 64

Industrial connectivity, 91

Industrial engineers, 53–55

Infinite Corridor, 13–23

Informational surround, 133–134

Innovations, lack of, 87

Interfaces, 135–136

Japanese Micromouse Association (JMA), 160

Jerome, Chauncey, 27

Jervis, John, 29

Jet engine technology, 70
Jobs, Steve, 133
John Wayne mentality, 19

Knee, prostheses for,
    118–127
Knowledge, categories of, 36
Kremer, Henry, 8–9

Language of science, 43–44
Learning
    from failures, 8, 9
    by machines, 157–171
Lettvin, Jerry, 89
Levine, Les, 131
Levy, Stephen, 105–106
Logical elements, relays for,
    98–101
Logical machines, 76
Logical puns, 18
Lowell, Mr., 36, 37

Machines
    learning by, 157–171
    vision for, 180–192
MacKenzie, John, 103
Maclaurin, Richard, 47,
    51–53, 56
MaCready, Paul, 9
Mann, Bob, 111–116
Manual training, 40–41
Manufacturers, graduates
    hired by, 42
Manufacturing,
    nanotechnology for, 146
Massachusetts Institute of
    Technology. *See* MIT
Matrix, corridors as, 60–61
Maze racing, 157–171

Mead, Carver, 177–188
Mechanical drawing, 109–111
Mechanical lab rat, 98, 158
Media Lab, 133–144
Mentor system, demise of, 42
Mice, maze racing by,
    157–171
Microprocessors, 87
Military research, 78–79
Milk, drop of, 173–175
Mill architects, 53–55
Mills, 30–31
Minds
    and nature, 191
    variety of, 43–45
Miniaturization, 145–156
Minski, Marvin, 105, 185–186
MIT
    corridors, 13–23, 54–57,
        59–60
    design of, 51–60
    early students at, 39–43
    move to Cambridge by,
        47–57
    opening of, 31–39
Mobility aid, 113
Model Railroad Club, 89–107
Modular elements in design,
    54–57
Molecular voltmeters,
    149–150
Molecules and
    nanotechnology, 145–156
Morison, Elting, 27–28
Motors for maze racing, 161
Move to Cambridge, 47–57
Movie Map, 134–135
Mugita, Kenji, 169–170
Music stand, self-paging, 2–7

Nanotechnology, 145–156
National Science Foundation
    (NSF), 122
Natural behavior of artifacts,
    79
Nature
    as artificial, 51
    and engineering, 11
    and minds, 191
Navigators, automated, 138
Negroponte, Nicholas,
    130–135, 141
Nerds, 82–86
Neurophysiology, 177–178
New mind, 43–45

Olsen, Ken, 116
Operating expenses, 80–81
Otten, Dave, 162–163,
    166–170
Owens, Francis, 34

Parts-oriented processes,
    16–17
Persig, Robert, 4–5
Photocells, molecular, 150
Physical truth, 36
Physics of parts, 16–17
"Plan for a Polytechnic School
    in Boston, A" (Rogers), 36
Polytechnic Institute of
    Karlsruhe, 40
Power
    for computers, 187
    for maze racing, 164–165
    for prostheses, 121
Practical experience, 40–41
Pritchett, Henry, 48
Problem-solving, 1–12

Processor simulators, 126
Productivity of engineering,
    87–88
Programming, 71
    animation simulations,
        142–143
    of cash register, 11–12
    courses for, 102
Prostheses, 112–114
    for elbows, 115–117
    for knees, 118–127
Psychology of wholes, 16–17
Puns, 18

Racing, maze, 157–171
Radar, invention of, 66–70
Radiation Lab, 66–70
    Model Railroad Club in,
        89–107
Radicalism, 129–130
Railroad club, 89–107
Rats, mechanical, 98, 158
Red Queen strategy, 81
Relays for model railroad,
    97–102
Reliability of relays, 99–100
Rensselaer Polytechnic, 40
Research, 78–79
Reservoirs, 29–31
Retina, modeling of, 179–192
Reverse beauty contests,
    84–85
Reverse engineering, 50
Rogers, Henry, 33, 35–36
Rogers, William Barton,
    32–39, 47

Sachs, Oliver, 118
Samson, Peter, 103, 104

Scale and nanotechnology, 145–156

Science
vs. art, 59
and educational reform, 34
language of, 43–44

Scientists
vs. engineers, 50
omnipotence attributed to, 78

Sculpture vs. tools, 58

Searching solution space, 7–8

Second Self, The (Turkle), 84

Self-assembling technologies, 152, 156

Self-paging music stand, 2–7

Sensors
and actuators, 73–74
molecular, 150, 154

Shannon, Claude, 98, 158–159

Sheet music turner, 2–7

Shop culture, 40–41

Simon, Herbert, 74

Simulations, 142–143

Simulators, 116–117, 126

Sinclair, Bruce, 83

Solution space, 1–12

Space Wars computer game, 105

Spatial Imaging Project (SIP), 138–144

Specifications, 17, 50

Sports, technical, 157–171

Square dances, 21–23

Staircases in maze racing, 169

Standley, David, 189–191

Steinmetz, Charles, 5

Strategy of collective systems, 180–182

Suicides, 19–20

Surface chemistry, 148–149

Surfing contest, MIT as, 18–19

Surgery, nanotechnology for, 146

"Swallowing the surgeon," 146

Synchronization of artificial knees, 118–119

System tools, 105

Taylor, Frederick Winslow, 41

Tech Model Railroad Club (TMRC), 89–107

Technical sports, 157–171

TechSquare dances, 21–23

Theroux, Alexander, 84n

3-D images, 138–144

Time-sharing program, 105

Tool art, 26

Tools
anonymity in design of, 58–59
discovery of, 25–26
investments in, 80
and nerds, 84
new, rate of, 87
system, 105
test of, 58
whole and parts of, 17

Trades, disdain for, 49

Train club, 89–107

Trial-and-error, 9

Truth
physical, 36
in structure, 28

Tucker, Carleton, 100, 106

Turing, Alan, 72–75

Turkle, Sherry, 84

Turner, sheet music, 2–7

TX-O computer, 103–104
Tying down molecules,
147–149

Ugliest man on campus
contests, 85
Unit-of-measure puns, 18

Variety of mind, 43–45
Virginia, University of, 35
Vision Chip Project, 188–192
Voltmeters, molecular,
149–150

Water projects, 29–31

Weisner, Jerome, 89, 136
West, Harry, 18
Whitney, Eli, 27
Whole-oriented processes,
16–17
Wiener, Norbert, 114–116
Wrighton Group, 149–156
Wrighton, Mark, 149, 150
Wyatt, John, 175–177,
182–183, 188, 190

Young Mechanic, 31

*Zen and the Art of Motorcycle
Maintenance* (Persig), 4–5